THE COMPLETE GUIDE TO SCHNAUZERS

Allison Hester

LP Media Inc. Publishing
For information address LP Media Inc. Publishing, 3178 253rd Ave. NW, Isanti, MN 55040
www.lpmedia.org

Publication Data

Schnauzers

The Complete Guide to Schnauzers – First edition.

Summary: "Successfully raising a Schnauzer Dog from puppy to old age" – Provided
by publisher.

ISBN: 978-1-952069-96-3

[1. Schnauzers – Non-Fiction] I. Title.

Design by Sorin Rădulescu

First paperback edition, 2020

TABLE OF CONTENTS

CHAPTER 1
Overview Of The Breed

What is a Schnauzer?

When people think of Schnauzers, the image that typically comes to mind is the adorable little silver dog with the charming bushy beard and eyebrows. This seems fitting since in German—where the breed originated—the word "Schnauzer" refers to the word "snout," and is a popular expression for "mustache" or "whiskered snout."

Beyond their celebrated looks, Schnauzers also are known for their temperaments. They are considered one of the smartest dog breeds because they are both easy to train and yet still able to think on their feet. They are awesome guard dogs, and extremely loving and loyal to their families.

FUN FACT
Miniature Schnauzers

The American Miniature Schnauzer Club (AMSC) recognizes three coat colors of Miniature Schnauzers: salt and pepper, black, and black and silver. While white Miniature Schnauzers are bred in the United States, they can't be shown in a conformation dog show.

I've been the owner of a rescued Miniature Schnauzer for nine years, and it's been an amazing experience. I have owned numerous dogs over my almost 50 years of life, but none have been as special to me as my Schnauzer. Funny, sweet, protective, and extremely loyal, she is truly a cherished member of our family.

Three Distinct Breeds

While most people think of Schnauzers as the miniature variety, there are actually three distinct breeds of Schnauzers: the Miniature Schnauzer, the Standard Schnauzer, and the Giant Schnauzer. The Standard Schnauzer was the original German version of the dog, and the Miniature and Giant were developed after crossbreeding to create the desired size and characteristics.

- The **Miniature Schnauzer** is an extremely popular dog, once listed as the third most popular breed by the American Kennel Club (AKC). As of the time of writing this book, the Miniature Schnauzer is 17th in popularity. Miniature Schnauzers are members of the terrier group, but they are not actually related. The AKC approves salt and pepper, black and silver, and solid black as acceptable coats. Miniature Schnauzers can also be pure white, but that is not an approved AKC color. Miniatures stand about one foot tall at the shoulder, weigh between 14 and 20 pounds, and typically live around 12 to 15 years.

- The **Standard Schnauzer** was the original version of the breed. These dogs stand around 1.5 feet tall and weigh between 30 to 50 pounds. Their wiry coats are either solid black or salt and pepper. Standard Schnauzers are members of the working dog group and were first bred in Germany to catch vermin and guard properties. They have also been used to carry mail in times of war, to support Red Cross efforts, and as police dogs. Today they are the least popular of the three breeds, rated 85th of 193 in breed popularity by the AKC. Standards typically live between 13 and 16 years.

- The **Giant Schnauzer** is the largest of the Schnauzer breeds, and it is quite the impressive beast. Standing over two feet high at the shoulder, and weighing up to 85 pounds, this muscular breed is a member of the working group. The Giant's double coat is either salt and pepper or solid black. These dogs are rated by the AKC as 79th in popularity out of 193 breeds. Giants typically live between 12 and 15 years.

*Photo Courtesy
of Ron Fazio*

History of the Schnauzer

The original Standard Schnauzer's history runs at least as far back as the Middle Ages in Germany. In the early days, dogs very similar to Standard Schnauzers were important assets around homes and farms. Standard Schnauzers were designed to be more than just working dogs. They were also important members of the family.

The early Schnauzers were descendants of other early European guarding and herding breeds. They protected farms from vermin, herded farm animals, and protected both livestock and their families. They could often be found accompanying their family members to market, where they loyally guarded their owners' carts.

Early Schnauzer coats came in a variety of colors, including tan, red, black, and parti-colored (i.e., black, white, and tan). Around the mid-1800s, Germans began crossbreeding the Standard Schnauzer with the black German Poodle, as well as the gray Wolfspitz to create the black and salt and pepper coat colors. The Standard Schnauzer was actually called the "Wire-Haired Pinscher" when first exhibited as a show dog in Germany in 1879, and a standard for the breed was first published in 1880. It wasn't until around 1900 that the breed became universally known as the "Schnauzer."

The AKC first recognized the Miniature Schnauzer as a member of the Terrier group in 1926—although the dogs had no Terrier in them. The breed grew in worldwide popularity after World War II and has been one of the most popular breeds since.

Giant Schnauzers came on the scene a little after the Miniatures by crossing the Standard with the black Great Dane and the Bouvier des Flandresto. As their name suggests, Giants were designed basically to be a bigger, hardier version of the Standard, handling many of the same tasks—helping farmers in several tasks, guarding property, and helping drive animals to market—but with a bit more gusto. They originated in the Bavarian Alps as cattle dogs. By the early 1900s, Giant Schnauzers also started having more modern roles such as watchdogs and military dogs during WWI and WWII.

Giant Schnauzers didn't make it to America until around 1930, and they were rarely seen in the US until the 1960s. Today, Giant Schnauzers are often used as police dogs in the US, and as carters (i.e., pulling carts filled with supplies) in other parts of the world.

Physical Characteristics

While the three breeds of Schnauzer vary by height, weight, and color, they all have some similar characteristics.

- Schnauzers have rectangular, strong heads, with a top-flat skull.
- They have small, dark brown eyes that are bright and perceptive,
- Their ears have traditionally been docked, but some breeders are getting away from this trend.
- Schnauzers also typically have docked tails. "Historically, the ears and tails were cropped and docked so that it would be harder for the rats to bite them and cause infection," explains Kelly Robison of Belle Vista Schnauzers, a professional Ohio-based breeder.
- They feature a double coat, which means a wiry outer coat, and a close, smooth undercoat.

All three breeds are muscular, and the Giants can be quite imposing. Even the Miniatures are thickset compared to many other small dogs.

Photo Courtesy
of Dagne Sereicikiene

nuo Bjauryb

5

Behavioral Characteristics

The original German version of the Schnauzer was a working dog who helped out in a variety of roles around the farm. Schnauzers served as watchdogs, ratters, hunters, protectors, as well as family companions.

Schnauzers were first bred to have both the sturdy build and the mental discernment to handle complex tasks and commands around the house and farm, as well as the confidence to step up and work independently when necessary. As a result, hundreds of years later, Schnauzers still need both physical and mental stimulation to be happy and to not act out.

Temperament

According to the AKC, Schnauzers should be "alert and spirited, yet obedient to command."

All three Schnauzer breeds are extremely smart dogs, but sometimes their high level of intelligence can be problematic. While Schnauzers can be easily trained, which is a positive, they also are smart enough to sometimes figure out "better ways" of doing things rather than obeying their owners' commands.

Because they are so smart, Schnauzers often get into mischief. For example, they may figure out how to get into cabinets or on top of tables in order to get to the things they want, or how to get out of a yard if the fence has a weak spot.

Schnauzers are also extremely loyal to their owners. They want to be involved in anything that their family is doing, and rarely want to be left alone. They live for their families. When we are gone, our Schnauzer religiously watches out the bedroom window, waiting for us to get home. Then she frantically greets us with high-pitched shrieks of joy when we arrive— whether we've been gone five hours or five minutes.

"Many people refer to them as 'Velcro dogs,'" explains Kelly Robison. "They really love their people and want to go where they go. Most owners of Miniature Schnauzers claim they've never gone to the bathroom alone since getting a Miniature Schnauzer. If you are up and moving around, they are right with you and can occasionally be a tripping hazard."

A Schnauzer's loyalty also means they are extremely protective of their families. No matter their size, Schnauzers boldly and confidently stand up to anyone or anything they think may put their family in harm's way. However, they typically aren't aggressive unless they sense their family is in harm's way. In my situation, my dog is very protective and leery of strangers when we are home, but not the slightest bit unfriendly or aggressive if we are somewhere else, like the dog park.

While some Schnauzers are friendly and sociable, others are timid or skittish around strangers and other dogs and may need more socialization than some other breeds. Still others are hyper and spirited, which means unless trained otherwise, they will jump on you—a lot. Also, because Schnauzers are so protective, some don't do well around children—or at least groups of children—especially if they are trying to protect a child in their household. For instance, my grandmother's Miniature Schnauzer would just bark and growl at me every time I visited as a child.

Finally, because they were bred to hunt rodents, some Schnauzers don't do well with cats or other small animals in the home. That depends on the dog, however. Mine was extremely gentle towards our guinea pigs, and our cat is her best friend. However, she will chase and kill any small animal she can catch out in our yard.

Again, Giant Schnauzers are mostly much larger versions of their smaller counterparts, so their behaviors will be similar to the Miniatures, only in a massive package. Giants may be too much for some households. They need their owners to be alphas, and then typically do well with consistent obedience training.

Finally, many Schnauzers are sensitive dogs and are keenly aware of their owner's moods. They will want to stay physically close, especially if they sense you are feeling down. Because they are so smart and loyal, Schnauzers can make good service and emotional support dogs if appropriately trained.

Photo Courtesy of Sarah LaGrone

Exercise Requirements

All three breeds have a lot of energy that needs to be burned off, or it could lead to destructive behavior. Without enough exercise, Schnauzers will find alternatives like chasing the kids, tearing up papers or shoes, digging in the yard, and getting in the middle of everything.

Regular walks are important, as is a yard or park where they can run, play, and chase small animals. "Most Miniature Schnauzers need some good exercise a couple times a day," adds Pat A. Hunt of Alpats Miniature Schnauzers. "A brisk walk is good, but playing a game of fetch in the yard is much better. They need their energy drained a couple times a day or they may chew or act out. Fetch inside is good too."

Because they are both smart and energetic, agility training is a great outlet as well for the enthusiastic owner because it provides both the physical and mental stimulation the dogs crave.

If you own a Schnauzer, a fenced yard is best as they tend to chase after any small animals they see. The same goes for using a leash when walking, as their ingrained hunting instincts might take over, no matter how well trained they may be.

Ultimately, as long as Schnauzers can get exercise, they adapt well to both city and country life. However, they generally need to be around their family as much as possible, not isolated in a backyard.

Grooming

Schnauzers shed minimally, which means they must be groomed, or their hair will get knotted up. As Kelly Robison explains, "They are touted as non-shedding, but no dog is truly non-shedding. The dead hairs don't release from the hair follicle in the same manner as a normally coated dog, but they do still lose hair. Often it is caught up in the other hair and can create mats instead of falling to the floor or sticking to your clothing. This is why keeping a Miniature Schnauzer regularly groomed is so important."

Schnauzers have a double coat, which means the top coat is wiry and the undercoat is soft. The breed standard calls for a hard, wiry coat. To achieve this, Schnauzers need to have their coats stripped at least two times a year—i.e., plucking loose, dead hairs—which will remove the undercoat and encourage the hard top coat to come in fuller. However, this is only really necessary if you want to achieve the breed standard for show dogs.

"The undercoat is what is promoted and seen in a shaved coat, but in a coat that is maintained as a 'rolled' or 'hand-stripped' coat, the outer coat is promoted and creates a hard, coarse texture," adds Kelly Robison. "The hard outer coat is more dirt resistant and easier to keep clean, but can often require weekly maintenance that differs from just brushing."

In addition to having your dog's hair cut, regular brushing will help keep a Schnauzer's coat shiny and healthy. It also can help improve your dog's circulation.

The Schnauzer cut consists of a tight cut along the neck, body, and tail. Miniature Schnauzers will have a skirt, with their legs left longer. Standard and Giant cuts are tighter around the entire body and don't feature a skirt. Then the face includes the trademark bushy beard and eyebrows.

Barking

Photo Courtesy of Chelsey Laughlin

Schnauzers are great watchdogs—perhaps to a fault. Unless they are properly trained, they will bark at "evildoers" (as my family calls them)—i.e., anyone who they think is getting too close to their family, even if it's neighbors who are way down the street. If allowed, they will stand guard over their households all day and night, which means you may be woken up in the middle of the night because of a neighborhood cat . This can be quite frustrating, although our Schnauzer did help catch some burglars breaking into neighborhood vehicles at 3 a.m. (Puggles is my hero!)

Schnauzers are not only excessive barkers; they are loud. Some Miniature Schnauzers also have a high-pitched squealing bark when they are excited, like when their family members arrive home. Warning: it can be quite shrill.

Is a Schnauzer the Right Fit for You?

With three distinct breeds, Schnauzers are good for small, medium, and large-sized dog lovers alike. Smart, loyal, friendly, and loving, Schnauzers make great family pets.

Photo Courtesy of Abby Terhark

However, there are things you need to consider before getting a Schnauzer.

1. Will you be able to provide the amount of exercise these high-energy dogs require?

2. Are you willing and able to invest in a Schnauzer's grooming needs?

3. Are you willing to put up with a dog that barks (or shrieks) excessively?

4. Can you handle a dog that wants to be in the middle of everything you do?

5. Do you want an inside dog? Schnauzers do not do well when left alone outside.

6. Do you have other pets? Some Schnauzers may not do well with cats or other animals.

Most importantly, do you have the time and willingness to properly train your Schnauzer? I volunteer at our local animal shelter, and the number one reason people relinquish their dogs is "no time to train."

Schnauzers are truly a blessing when it comes to training as, again, they are super smart, and often easier to train than most breeds. But they can't learn what they aren't taught. That's the goal of this book—to help you have the best possible experience with your Schnauzer.

CHAPTER 2
Choosing a Schnauzer

When it comes to choosing your Schnauzer, you have a few options. One of the biggest things to consider is whether to buy a Schnauzer from a breeder or adopt from a rescue.
Here are some things to consider:

- Which breed of Schnauzer do you want—Miniature, Standard, or Giant?
- How much do you want to spend on purchasing your dog?
- Do you want to breed your Schnauzer?
- Do you want to show your Schnauzer?
- How important is it for you to have a purebred dog?
- Do you want a puppy or an older dog?
- Do you have a heart for rescue animals?

Breeders vs. Rescues

Let's start with some advantages of buying from breeders:

1. You know the dog's history. A breeder can tell you all about the puppy's life: how she was raised, any health concerns, personality, etc.
2. You can learn about the puppy's parents. This can give you insights into potential health issues as well as temperament.
3. You know how the puppy was raised. When buying from a reputable breeder, you don't have to worry that the puppy has been neglected or abused. With a rescue, you don't know the dog's history and how that might impact its behavior.
4. You can check the breeder's references. This can give you an idea about other satisfied customers.
5. You can get expert advice about your Schnauzer from the breeder before you purchase.
6. If raised by a reputable breeder, your Schnauzer should meet the breed's standards.
7. Your Schnauzer will likely have a health guarantee. This means the breeder may provide a refund should the dog come down with a disease covered by the agreement.

8. The breeder can help you choose the best puppy for you.

9. You will be able to contact the breeder with questions for years to come.

10. You may be able to return your puppy if you are not happy.

Miniature Schnauzers from breeders cost around $3,000 on average. Giant Schnauzers can range from $1,300 to over $5,000 a puppy, depending on pedigree. Standards Schnauzers run around $1,500.

Photo Courtesy of Sarah LaGrone

Now let's look at adopting a Schnauzer.

- Adopting through a rescue gives a needy Schnauzer a second chance, and in some cases, even saves its life.
- Rescued Schnauzers are generally significantly less expensive than purchasing from a breeder.

If your heart is set on a purebred Schnauzer, but you don't want to spend the cost associated with breeders, there may be rescue options that can still provide AKC paperwork. Full-blooded Schnauzers can end up in rescues for a number of reasons that are no fault of their own. Owners die, become too ill to care for their dogs, relocate, get divorced, and so on. These Schnauzers need loving homes too.

A Schnauzer found as a stray will not come with AKC paperwork. The dog may still be a full-blooded Schnauzer, or she may be a mix. Before considering a rescue, you need to decide how important having a full-blooded Schnauzer is to you. My dog, for example, was found as a stray. While she definitely looks like she could be a purebred Miniature Schnauzer, I don't know for certain, but that doesn't matter to me.

Full-blooded Schnauzer rescues are almost always going to be a little older. Rescue groups do sometimes have puppies, but those will likely be mixed Schnauzer breeds unless they were rescued from a puppy mill. If they came from a puppy mill, they still need good homes, but just know that their quality of breeding will likely not be as high as if they came from a reputable breeder, and there may be some unexpected health issues.

Another possible option is getting a slightly older puppy that was returned to a breeder. The reasons for returning a dog to a breeder vary but may be anything from allergies to not having the time to properly train. When this happens, you can usually get the returned Schnauzer at a discounted price.

How to Find a Reputable Breeder

"You want your breeder to belong to a national breed club like 'The American Miniature Schnauzer Club', or a local club like 'The Portland Miniature Club', this is just an example and may vary by state. We also have all breed clubs and just terrier clubs they can belong to as well. The reason behind that is because in order to join they sign a Code of Ethics stating they will uphold to these standards of the breed and be honest."

RHONDA SMITH
Heavenly Miniature Schnauzer

When it comes to buying a Schnauzer puppy from a breeder, there are good breeders and bad ones. When searching for a breeder, you ideally want to find one that you can meet with in person. Here's why:

- You can meet the puppy's mother (and possibly the father) in order to get a better idea of appearance and temperament.

Photo Courtesy of Chelsey Laughlin

- You can see what kind of conditions the puppies were raised in and how they were treated by the breeder. Puppies should be raised inside as part of the family, not left outside in kennels.
- You can watch how the breeder interacts with the puppies to see if they are happy and healthy.
- You can see the cleanliness of the premises where they were raised, and the cleanliness and health of the puppies.

If you are looking at a breeder that is out of your area, you can still ask questions, ask for referrals from both customers and veterinarians, and require the breeder to provide the appropriate paperwork.

Photo Courtesy
of Deborah Holmes

Here are a few more things to consider when selecting a breeder:

A quality breeder:
- is available to answer your questions about the training and care of your puppy long after your puppy goes home
- doesn't require you to use a specific veterinarian if you choose to have the puppy checked out before you purchase it
- never sells to pet stores
- only breeds limited types of dogs and does not have litters available at all times.

A quality breeder should also interview you to make sure the puppy is going to a good home. They will provide you with a written contract and health guarantee. Some breeders will require you to sign paperwork stating you will return the dog to them if you can't keep her so they can rehome the dog themselves to ensure she goes to a good home.

Health Tests and Certifications

"If a breeder won't allow you to visit the puppies and meet the mom and dad, be cautious. A breeder should be willing to allow you to see the conditions your puppy will be raised in for the first eight weeks."

TIMOTHY SWAIN
Swains Sweet Schnauzers

A quality breeder will be happy to provide you with proof of any health tests for the puppy's parents, as well as the puppy's shot record and veterinarian visits. They will also have solid relationships with at least one veterinarian.

For Miniature Schnauzers, Kelly Robison offers this advice: "Make sure both parents have had the minimum recommended health testing for the breed, which includes eye exams performed by a board-certified veterinary ophthalmologist, a cardiac exam by a board-certified veterinary cardiologist, and genetic testing for myotonia congenita and mycobacterium avium complex (MAC). The whole litter should be checked by a board-certified veterinary ophthalmologist before leaving for new homes."

The AKC has specific health tests that are required for various breeds. When it comes to Schnauzers, the tests vary by breed, but all three need to have an eye examination by a board-certified ACVO ophthalmologist. Additional tests are as follows:

- **Miniature Schnauzers** require a cardiac evaluation. Optional tests include myotonia congenita and mycobacterium avian complex.
- **Standard Schnauzers** need to be tested for hip dysplasia and have a dilated cardiomyopathy test. Cardiac evaluations, autoimmune thyroiditis, and a DNA repository are optional.
- **Giant Schnauzers** require tests for autoimmune thyroiditis and hip dysplasia.

If you are purchasing an official AKC breed, the breeder should provide you with an AKC registration application that is clearly labeled with the AKC logo and the words "American Kennel Club" on it. A breeder should never ask you to pay for the papers, refuse to give you the papers, or say the papers will be sent to you later.

Breeder Contracts and Guarantees

A breeder will require you to sign a contract that lays out what is expected of both of you. The contract will include facts about the puppy, such as its registration numbers, parents, date of birth, etc. It will also include information on the sales price, and any specifics about expectations and/or a current balance if you are paying in installments.

Breeders also often include a guarantee stating that your puppy is healthy at the time you purchase her. You will be required to take the puppy to a veterinarian within a specific time period to confirm the puppy is in good health. The contract may also outline any health guarantees that the breeder provides for genetic conditions and what your responsibility is if these conditions arise.

A breeder may have some additional requirements for purchasing a puppy. If you purchase a show-quality puppy, the breeder may expect you to show your dog. Or, if you purchase a female, you may be required to breed her and give the breeder one of the puppies.

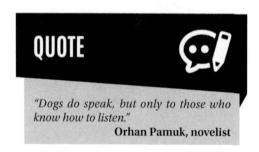

QUOTE

"Dogs do speak, but only to those who know how to listen."
Orhan Pamuk, novelist

Requirements vary by breeder, so it's important to read the contract carefully prior to signing, and if there's something you don't agree with, you may want to find a different breeder. Just know that if you've already paid a deposit, you may not be able to get it back.

Choosing the Perfect Pup

Puppies usually stay with their mother until they are at least eight weeks old, while their mother teaches them proper manners. Don't choose a breeder who wants to rehome puppies before then. Quality breeders don't always have puppies available, and they often have a waiting list.

The litter size will vary by breed:

- Miniature Schnauzers: 3 to 6 puppies
- Standard Schnauzers: 6 to 10 puppies
- Giant Schnauzers: 5 to 8 puppies

A quality breeder will have hand-raised the puppies and will know their individual personalities. This can help the breeder determine which puppy will be the best fit for your family's specific wants and needs.

You will also want to make sure the puppy is healthy. Again, the breeder should provide you with health records, but you will want to examine the pup yourself. Here are some things to look for:

1. Schnauzers should look well-fed but not have a distended belly, which could be a sign of worms.

2. Eyes should be clear and bright, with no discharge.

3. Ears should be clean, with no dirty buildup or discharge. You can check hearing by quickly making a not-too-loud noise, like clapping your hands, while the dog is distracted and see if she responds.

4. Noses should be cool and clean without discharge.

5. Gums should be clean and healthy pink.

6. Coats should be clean and shiny.

7. Skin should not be red or irritated, and there should be no bald spots, which may be a sign of a skin problem or fleas and ticks.

8. The puppy should breathe clearly, with no wheezing or coughing.

Photo Courtesy of Jeff Rangel

Tips for Adopting a Schnauzer

If you choose to go the adoption route, you will not have the guarantees that you have from a breeder, and you may or may not have paperwork depending on how the dog became a rescue.

Photo Courtesy
of Merry Morrissy-Karp

Shelters are full of wonderful dogs, and they do occasionally get some Schnauzers or Schnauzer mixes. In my experience as a volunteer at our local shelter, small breeds and "designer dogs"—including all types of Schnauzers—go quickly. Unless a dog was relinquished by the original owner, the shelter won't know a lot about the animal, including whether she's a purebred or a mix. When it comes to things like age, breed, potty training, and whether a dog is good with kids, cats, or other dogs—these are also all guesses. Shelter volunteers can only tell you what they've observed.

If you are considering a dog from the shelter, ask to take her outside. This may give you a better idea of the dog's personality. Keep in mind that dogs often act very differently after being adopted than they did at the shelter. That's because a shelter is often loud and scary. Dogs who are shy at the shelter often warm up quickly once they find their new forever family, and hyper shelter dogs often calm down.

It's important to realize that animal shelters have limited resources. They may not test for things like heartworms unless there is a specific reason, and they usually only have a vet check the dogs if there's cause for concern. Unlike breeders, shelters do not offer health guarantees. They will, however, give shots and spay or neuter.

Rescue groups may be able to provide more details, depending on whether a dog was relinquished or found as a stray. Many rescue groups rely on foster homes that keep the dogs until they are adopted, which means the foster parents get a better feel for the dog's temperament than a shelter would.

When buying from a rescue group, expect to complete a detailed application and to possibly have a volunteer visit your home to make sure the house and yard are a good fit for a Schnauzer. They want to make sure that the rescued Schnauzer is not returned to the shelter—traumatic for any dog—and that both your home and yard are adequate for the breed's needs.

Shelters and rescue groups alike will require you to fill out an application, which will ask questions about your living situation, history with animals, etc. If you have other pets, you will have to show proof that they are up-to-date on vaccinations. If you are a renter, the shelter may want a copy of the rental agreement or could contact your landlord to make sure you are allowed to have pets.

The shelter or rescue may offer a free trial period where you can bring the dog back if things don't work out. Additionally, most rescue groups will require that, if things don't work out, you agree to return the dog to foster care rather than taking her to a kill shelter.

CHAPTER 3
Preparing Your Home for Your Schnauzer

Bringing your new Schnauzer home is an exciting time, but it's not easy. Introducing a new dog to her home is a lot of work, especially a high-energy Schnauzer puppy. Dogs get returned or surrendered all the time because families get a cute little puppy then realize they don't have the time and energy required to properly care for her. The more you can do to prepare your home and family, the more successful your transition will be. If you are bringing home a puppy, you need to ideally spend about a month preparing your home beforehand.

Photo Courtesy of Louize Carpio

Preparing Your Kids

Your kids will likely be spending a lot of time with your new Schnauzer, so you need to make sure they know how to interact with your new dog. It's best to have rules defined before your Schnauzer arrives.

1. **Play gently** – Young children, especially, tend to be a little rough when it comes to petting and handling a new pet. Your new Schnauzer will likely be excited to be with her new family, but she may be a little anxious as well. Don't let your children rush over to the new dog. It's best to let the new dog come over to the child, not vice versa. Help your children gently pet their new Schnauzer, preferably starting on the back because it's less intrusive. With very young children, you can use a stuffed animal to practice on prior to bringing the dog home.

   Always keep an eye on your younger children when they are interacting with your new dog until they are completely comfortable with each other. Puppies, in particular, will start to nip and bite if playtime gets too excited or rough. The next thing you know, your child gets nipped, cries, and is afraid of the dog, but it's not the puppy's fault. She has to be trained.

2. **Respect the dog's warning signs** – Children need to be taught to recognize if the new dog is uncomfortable with their behavior. Dogs will generally give warning signs that they are not happy. These include growling, walking away, not wanting to be held, hiding, and so on. Teach your children to respect the dog's behavior and give it some space. Otherwise the dog may become anxious around your kids.

3. **Don't touch the Schnauzer when she is eating** – Dogs can feel defensive if they feel like they are fighting for their food.

4. **Carefully hold the Schnauzer** – Children need to learn how to properly hold the new puppy or dog, or it can be very uncomfortable for the Schnauzer. For younger children, it may be best to implement a no-holding rule until they are older. It can be difficult for little children to hold a squirming dog, and the frustrated dog may nip or bite.

5. **Keep valuables out of the dog's reach** – Puppies, in particular, like to chew on things they aren't supposed to because they are teething. If a puppy destroys your child's favorite stuffed animal, it's not the dog's fault. The toy should have been kept out of reach.

6. **No hitting!** – If the new dog nips, your child's first impulse may be to spank or hit the dog. Let your children know that hitting the dog is never acceptable. (We'll talk more about training in Chapter 10.)

Preparing Your Other Dogs

If you already have a dog (or dogs), introducing the new Schnauzer into the household can be another challenge. If your current dog knows how to interact with other dogs without problems, you will probably not have a big issue. However, if your dog tends to be territorial or doesn't get along well with other dogs, then you're going to need to use caution and patience when introducing your new Schnauzer to the family.

Photo Courtesy of Abigail Colbert

Some dogs are fine in most situations but can become territorial when it comes to their own house. My Schnauzer is great with other dogs at the dog park. We have also fostered a few dogs at our house, and while she does well, for the most part, she gets grumpy when it comes to rawhides. She will let the other dogs eat her food, but if they try to steal her rawhide, she snaps at them.

You may need to keep your dog and the new Schnauzer

FUN FACT
Giant Schnauzer

Giant Schnauzers have a long history as working dogs. They were originally bred as agricultural dogs to drive cattle from farm to market in southern Germany. Later, they were commonly trained as military and police dogs. In modern times, Giant Schnauzers are known for their loyalty and intelligence and continue to serve as working dogs.

separated for a bit. Don't leave the dogs alone together without supervision until you're sure they will get along okay. The best option is to initially set up a separate space for your new dog (as discussed later).

Before bringing your puppy home, it's best to let your current dog(s) meet the new Schnauzer for the first time somewhere outside of your home on neutral ground, such as at a park. This will help your dog not feel territorial when she meets the new Schnauzer, and they can get to know each other a little. You should have both dogs on leashes at first and have them approach each other slowly. The alpha of your family should control your current dog, and another family member should oversee the new Schnauzer.

This introductory period may go smoothly, or it may take some time based on your dog's personality. Don't be discouraged if it takes a week or even longer for your current dog and new Schnauzer to get acclimated. You are changing your home's dynamic, and just like people, dogs aren't always fans of change. Older dogs, especially, may have a hard time welcoming a new dog or puppy, and your dog may take its frustration out on the new Schnauzer. Do your best to make both dogs feel loved and accepted.

While you want to use caution when introducing dogs, some things will need to be hashed out between the dogs. Obviously, you don't want a grown dog attacking a puppy and hurting her, but an occasional growl or even snap at the puppy from your older dog is not necessarily bad. Dogs have a pecking order, and they each need to know where they stand.

Dangerous Things that Dogs Might Eat

There are certain human foods that can be dangerous for dogs, so before you bring your new Schnauzer home, you need to make sure that your family members, including children, know not to ever offer the following things as treats.

- **Chocolate** – Theobroma cacao is poisonous to dogs. The darker the chocolate, the more dangerous
- **Onions, garlic, chives, and other members of the lily family.** These contain thiosulfate, which dogs can't digest, and can make the dog anemic. Onions contain more thiosulfate than garlic.
- **Grapes and raisins** – Not all dogs have a reaction to grapes or raisins, but when they do, even one raisin can be toxic to a 10-pound dog. It's best not to take any chances and ever try feeding these, as just one reaction could be lethal.
- **Beans** – These can cause gas, diarrhea, and vomiting
- **Cooked bones and thin bones (like chicken)** – You have to be cautious with most bones because they can splinter and puncture the GI tract
- **Corn on the cob** – Corn is okay; cobs are not.
- **Grease and fat** – Schnauzers are prone to pancreatitis, and so avoiding high calorie, fatty foods is best.
- **Peaches, persimmons, and plums** – The pits contain cyanide, which is poisonous.
- **Avocados** – These contain a toxin called persin. The seed, skin, and leaves are the most dangerous parts of the avocado, but the fruit is also dangerous and should never be fed to a dog.
- **Caffeine** – This can be fatal to dogs.
- **Xylitol (a sugar substitute)** – This can cause a dog's blood sugar to drop, as well as lead to liver failure.
- **Yeast Dough** – The dough will continue to rise while in your dog's stomach, which can be painful. It can also lead to alcohol poisoning.
- **Alcohol** – Remember, your dog's metabolism is different from yours. Some people think it's funny to give their dogs alcohol, but it's actually dangerous and cruel.
- **Macadamia Nuts** – This can lead to symptoms such as muscle shakes, high fever, vomiting, and weakness.

Photo Courtesy
of Claudia Dancila

Other Household Dangers

"It is very similar to having a toddler in your house. Pick up all cords, electronics, battery operated toys, etc. from the floor and keep them out of reach. Never leave a puppy loose and unattended in the house. Crate training is your best friend."

KELLY ROBISON
Belle Vista Schnauzers

Having a puppy is a lot like having a toddler. They will get into anything they can get their teeth on. The following is a list of things you should check your house for before bringing home your new dog.

- **Cleaning supplies and poisons** – Schnauzers are smart, resourceful dogs and can often figure out how to get to what they want if it's not locked down. You probably should add childproof locks on your kitchen and bathroom cabinets, and definitely make sure you keep all poisons and cleaning problems locked away. Dogs often like the taste of rat poison, which can be deadly.

- **Trash can** – I have yet to find a bathroom trash can that my Schnauzer cannot get into. Anything you put in the trash can may be pulled back out by an unsupervised Schnauzer. Your best bet is to lock the can away in an area the dog cannot access.

- **Electrical cords** – Puppies like to chew on everything, electric cords included. You need to make sure they are kept up and away from where your new Schnauzer will have access, or you may have broken items pulled off the countertops, or worse, an electrocuted pup.

- **Blind cords and other long ropes or strings** – Keep these up and out of reach of your Schnauzer to prevent strangulation.

- **Avoid automatic toilet cleaners** – While you may usually keep toilet lids down, at some point, you might forget, and your dog might drink out of the toilet. When she does, you don't want the Schnauzer to consume dangerous cleaning products.

- **Tables** – Don't leave anything dangerous on tables like scissors, knives, pens, etc., as your Schnauzer may climb up to get ahold of them.

- **Litter boxes** – If you have a cat, keep the litter box where the dog cannot reach it, or get one that is designed to keep dogs out. Doing this before the new Schnauzer gets there is best so your cat is used to the change before dealing with the added stress of a new dog.

- **Clean up the garage** – It's especially important to clean up any anti-freeze leaks from the pavement and prevent any new ones. Dogs like the taste, and even a small amount can be fatal.

Photo Courtesy of Dana Stettin

Preparing an Inside Space for Your Schnauzer

Photo Courtesy of Kathryn Daniels

Before your new dog arrives home, you should figure out a safe, cleanable area that can be set up especially for your Schnauzer. Being in a new home will be stressful for your new dog, and even if she is already potty trained, there may be some accidents. The best option is to choose a section of your home that has hard flooring, not carpet. If you only have carpeted areas, then be sure to put down plenty of puppy pads or newspapers.

Confining your dog to one or two rooms at first is best. This lets your puppy safely explore and makes it easier for you to clean up after accidents.

Here are some of the things you'll need to purchase and set up before bringing your Schnauzer home:

- A crate
- A dog bed (choose one that is difficult to tear apart)
- A collar, leash, and/or harness with tags containing name and contact information
- Food and water bowls
- Dog or puppy food
- Grooming accessories (shampoo, brush, toothbrush, etc.)
- Toys
- Training treats
- Baby/dog gates if you need to keep your dog from going into certain parts of your home
- Potty pads for when you aren't home to potty train
- Enzymatic cleaners in case of accidents.

If you have children, you need to set up a child-free space where your dog can play with toys or eat a chew without being approached. A crate is usually a good option. We'll talk about crate training in Chapter 5, but for now, just know that a crate is a powerful way to make your new dog feel safe.

Preparing an Outside Space for Your Schnauzer

Before your new Schnauzer comes home, you need to take a careful look at your yard to make sure it is puppy- or dog-proof.

1. **Inspect the fence** – Look for holes or breaks where your dog could slip out, as well as protruding objects, such as nails.

   When we first got our Mini Schnauzer, our back gate was not properly installed, and she figured out how to crawl under it. We didn't realize it was a problem because we previously had two beagles who never messed with the gate. Then when we moved to a new house two years ago, our Schnauzer found a spot to slip out between the house and the side gate. In both situations, we thought we'd thoroughly inspected the yard and fence, but obviously we didn't do a good enough job. It's a horribly scary feeling when your dog gets out of the yard. When it comes to your new Schnauzer, it's best not to leave her outside alone until you have confirmed evidence (months of no escapes) that your yard is escape-proof.

2. **Remove any chemicals or other dangers** – You may have tools, gasoline, bug spray, lighter fluid, etc., on your back porch, deck, etc. You need to put these away in a place that your dog cannot access.

3. **Remove or blockade dangerous plants** – Your new dog may chew on any plants or flowers you have in your yard, so you need to make sure they are not poisonous. Several types of popular flowers and plants, such as tomato plants, holly, azaleas, daffodils, and others, can be poisonous to dogs. Do your research.

4. **Mow the yard** – Before your new pup comes home, make sure your grass is trimmed. This will keep your dog cleaner and will help keep fleas and ticks at bay.

5. **Set up a water station** – Your dog needs to have access to water outside, even if she will only be outside sporadically. Water should ideally be kept in a shady area, and you should make sure your dog knows where to get a drink. Keep the water bowl clean and full.

6. **Create potty zones** – If you want to keep your backyard cleaner, you can train your dog to only use a specific area as a bathroom. Determine where you want the dog to go potty before bringing her home, then begin training for that right away.

7. **Provide shelter if needed** – If you are going to allow your dog to stay outside when you aren't home, you should provide a doghouse. However, it's best not to leave a new puppy outside alone until she's a little older.

CHAPTER 4
Bringing Your Schnauzer Home

"A Schnauzer is as much at home in the city with a small amount of exercise as he is in the country where he appears tireless. And, he easily adapts to any change of condition or climate. His deepest need, however, is to live as a part of the family, going where they go, doing what they do. Sleeping on the bed, or in his own, beside his owner is his greatest joy."

RHONDA SMITH
Heavenly Miniature Schnauzer

Photo Courtesy of Ann Schuh

I n the last chapter we started talking about getting your home ready for your new Schnauzer. Now it's time to talk about bringing your new dog home and getting her settled in with you and your family. This will go more smoothly if you have a plan in place before you pick up your Schnauzer.

The Car Ride Home

Try to pick up your new Schnauzer on a day when you will be able to be home with her for at least 24 hours, like a weekend. If it's a weekday, it's best to take the following day off work if possible.

Sometimes people get a new dog from a shelter or breeder in their area, but it's not unusual for people to travel hours from home for their new Schnauzer either. Whether the ride home is five minutes or five hours, it's best to be prepared.

Before you start heading home, make sure you have all the paperwork from the dog breeder or rescue group. Find out what food the dog has been eating to try to keep stomach issues to a minimum. Try to get your new dog to go potty outside before getting in the car.

On the drive home, you'll need several items, including a crate or a box to carry the puppy home. You'll also want blankets or towels in the box, a collar or harness, and a leash. Bring treats and toys if it's going to be a long drive home.

Your best option—especially on a long drive—is to put your new Schnauzer in a crate. This will keep your new dog from climbing around the car, which can be dangerous both for the dog and everyone in the car. For one, your new dog may want to climb on the driver's lap or under the driver's feet, both of which are an accident waiting to happen. A crate is also safer for both you and your new Schnauzer in case of sudden stops, sharp turns, etc.

Crates also help control messes if your dog is excited and goes potty or if she gets nauseous during the car ride. Between nerves and motion, it's not uncommon for a dog to become car sick. Place puppy

HELPFUL TIP
Leash Laws

A leash may be one of your first purchases before bringing home a new dog. Leash laws vary widely from state to state, or even between counties or parks. In some areas, there are laws restricting the length of your dog's leash to ensure that you maintain control of your dog at all times. The use of retractable leashes is banned in some areas of the United States and Canada, so be sure to check the laws in your local area before deciding which type of leash is best for you and your pet.

Photo Courtesy
of Jeff Rangel

pads on the bottom of the crate, then add an old towel or blanket to make your new dog more comfortable. Just make sure to choose a towel that you don't mind throwing away in case of an accident or car sickness.

If your new dog is a puppy, you can also use a box if no crate is available. It's best to bring someone with you to ensure the puppy does not jump out of the box. Line the box with puppy pads under some towels or blankets, etc., in case of an accident.

If you don't have access to a crate and the dog is too big for a box, the next best option is to have someone sit with the Schnauzer in the back seat to keep her company and prevent her from getting up front and distracting the driver. Cover the seat with a blanket, as well as the floorboards, in case your dog is more comfortable there. You might place puppy pads there as well.

You want the car ride home to be as comforting for your new dog as possible. Don't be surprised, though, if your dog cries or barks during the car ride. Try to keep her fear minimized by staying calm. Soft music can be soothing as well.

If you have a long drive home, make sure you take plenty of breaks to let your new Schnauzer go potty and work off some energy. However, if your dog has not been fully vaccinated, don't stop at rest stops since other dogs have likely used the bathroom there and may have carried diseases.

The First Night Home

Hopefully your dog will arrive home early in the day so she has time to get used to being in your house before bedtime. As tempting as it may be to take your new dog for a big outing or invite friends and family over, it's best to try to limit activity and keep things relaxed so your new Schnauzer has a chance to unwind. Try to keep the house calm and low-key.

When the puppy enters your home, calmly let her sniff and roam around any areas where she's allowed to go. She may be hyper, or she may be timid as she roams. The important thing is that you stay calm and relatively quiet. If you have a yard, you'll want her to go outside and explore (and potty) shortly after exploring the house.

As she gets a feel for the house, she'll start to calm down. It's important to give your new dog her own safe space, where she can go if she feels overwhelmed. Again, a crate with a blanket and toys is a great option. You can leave the door to the crate open during the day so she can go in or come out on her own time.

When it's time for bed, again, a crate is your best option. You can even put the crate in your bedroom with you. If you don't have a crate, you can place a dog bed in the dog's designated closed-off area. Or, if you want, you can allow your dog to sleep in your bedroom. Just know that if you let the dog sleep on your bed, your new dog will expect to sleep there always. As tempting as it may be, your bed is not always the best option, especially with puppies, who will likely make a mess in your room.

If your dog isn't sleeping with you, expect her to cry the first few nights. One thing that can help is putting an old T-shirt you've worn in the crate or bed, so she has your scent. You may also want to leave a small light on. While the puppy is really young, go ahead and put water in the crate at night. Just know her bladder is going to get full quickly.

Your pup may be lonely, or she may have to use the bathroom. Young puppies, especially, have to use the bathroom every few hours. Take your dog out to use the bathroom as necessary in the middle of the night, then soothe her for a minute. If you show too much attention to her cries, though, you're actually reinforcing negative behavior. As hard as it may seem, a better option is to give a firm "quiet," then leave your pup alone. Just be sure you are consistent in your response.

Once you and your new Schnauzer get through the first night, take your pup out to potty as soon as you get up. It may be better to carry your puppy, to prevent an accident on the way outside. (We will get into potty training in Chapter 6.)

Expect the first night or two to be kind of rough, but take comfort in knowing that with a little bit of time and patience, your dog will soon recognize and accept bedtime.

First Vet Visit/Choosing a Vet

Whether you've gotten your dog from a breeder or a rescue, your new Schnauzer is likely up-to-date on her shots. A breeder may have had some other tests done to guarantee the dog's health against certain diseases. A rescue most likely has already had your new dog spayed or neutered or has required you to sign paperwork agreeing that you will have the procedure done within a certain time frame.

After you've gotten your new Schnauzer home, you should find a veterinarian and take your new dog in for a quick checkup.

When looking for a vet, consider:

1. How far is the vet from your home? You'll want a place that is relatively close.
2. Is the clinic accredited by the American Animal Hospital Association (AAHA)?
3. Has the veterinarian maintained his or her certifications from the American Board of Veterinary Practitioners (ABVP)?

Photo Courtesy
of Alice Vaccaro

4. What do other people say about the veterinarian or clinic? Social media makes it easy to look for recommendations from others in your area.

5. Is the clinic capable of processing tests and taking X-rays on-site?

6. What are the clinic's rates, and how do those compare to others in the area?

7. What is the veterinarian's communications style? You probably won't be able to determine this until after you've visited (although you may get feedback from others). Are the vets and staff friendly? Does the vet take time to answer your questions, or does s/he seem rushed? Is the vet able to effectively explain procedures, recommendations, etc.?

8. What is the wait time for appointments?

9. What are the vet's hours? Are they open on weekends?

10. Do they have emergency hours or a backup clinic?

11. How does overnight care work?

Shortly after your new Schnauzer arrives home, set up your dog's first veterinarian appointment. Your vet will likely want to set you up on heart-worm medicine and possibly flea and tick treatment. Also, your vet may tell you some things to keep an eye out for with your new Schnauzer.

Puppy Classes

With all the information available on the Internet that can show you how to teach a dog basic obedience commands, puppy classes may seem like a waste of time and money. However, even if you are an expert at "sit" and "stay," puppy classes offer many benefits that your puppy simply can't get at home with your family alone.

Just as important as training your puppy to follow some simple commands, puppy classes give your new Schnauzer pup an opportunity to socialize with other dogs and people. Studies have found that socializing your puppy will help her become more self-assured and acclimated when she is older. It will also help reduce future behavior issues like separation anxiety, fear responses, and biting.

Interestingly, your pup's behavior is not the only one that will improve. Studies have also found that dog owners who participate in puppy classes act more positively toward their puppy, rewarding their dog's good behavior as opposed to punishing, which often backfires. This positive reinforcement also helps create a stronger bond and trust between your dog and your family.

Not all puppy-training classes are created equal. When choosing a puppy class, select one that not only teaches some basic commands but also allows your puppy to interact and play with the other puppies in the class. You can find these at your local pet store or through professional dog trainers in your area.

Another important element that is often excluded in puppy classes is "resource-guarding" classes. This teaches dogs to share toys, food, treats, and so on.

Photo Courtesy
of Abigail Colbert

Some classes also cover important exposure training that slowly introduces the puppies to scary noises, weird smells, new sights, etc. This is another element that can be extremely valuable.

Before you sign up for a puppy class, ask to see the full curriculum. Ask if your Schnauzer will be exposed to supervised interaction with the other puppies and their owners, and inquire whether you can observe a class to see how it is conducted. Then pay particular attention to whether positive reinforcement is practiced and how more aggressive puppies are handled during playtime.

Preparing Your Bank Account

A lot of times, people don't realize how much their new dog is actually going to cost. While your dog will undoubtedly bring joy and fulfillment to your household, it's important to recognize that owning a dog may be more expensive than you think.

According to the American Society for the Prevention of Cruelty to Animals, you can expect to spend between $1,314 to $1,843—or more—in the first year of dog ownership. This includes some one-time expenses, such as puppy-training classes, a crate, leashes, a dog bed, food, and spaying and neutering.

After the first year, the ASPCA estimates your Schnauzer will cost an average of $580 to $875 (larger breeds typically cost more due to food consumption). This probably does not include emergency vet bills, for which you may want to set money aside.

About two years ago, my dog went out to potty about 10 p.m. and started screaming like I'd never heard. She had been bitten by a copperhead. At the emergency vet, they gave us two options. One was basically Benadryl and antibiotics—$300—and the other was antivenom, which was going to be $1,400–$2,800. We had to opt for the cheaper option, and fortunately, she was fine. My point, however, is that things unexpectedly happen, and it can be expensive, leading to some difficult choices if you're not financially prepared.

One option to consider is pet insurance. The cost of pet insurance depends on where you live, the age of your dog, the type of dog, and the type of coverage. However, on average, you can expect to pay around $500 a year on pet insurance, plus a deductible. Getting insurance early is smart, particularly if your dog develops conditions that would not enable her to qualify for insurance later in life.

If you don't want to pay for insurance, another recommended option is to set aside money in a special pet savings account. For this, determine how

Photo Courtesy
of Chelsey Laughlin

much extra you can afford to place in the account each month, and add to the account monthly until you reach your dedicated savings goal. This is a great way to put money aside in case you are faced with a tough, expensive decision that may make the difference between the life or death of your precious Schnauzer.

CHAPTER 5
Being a Schnauzer Parent

"It takes time for a puppy to assimilate to new people and surroundings. Eating can become concerning if they were only recently weaned. If they aren't eating put a little softened Kibble and pour some Esbalac over it. This will get your puppy back to eating quickly."

LINDA RODES
Sedor Kennel

When you think of bringing a new Schnauzer home, you probably envision only happy images like belly rubs, long walks in the park, and rainy-day cuddles. And yes, your new Schnauzer should bring you and your family years of joy...if you set things up for success right from the start.

*Photo Courtesy
of Sarah LaGrone*

For the greatest success, you should begin training your new Schnauzer the moment she becomes yours (if not before). Setting the tone, establishing ground rules, and practicing consistency from the get-go will help minimize problems.

Let's take a deeper look at some of the more common things you need to know as the parent of a new dog or puppy.

Crate Training

To some, crate training may seem unkind, but it's recommended by many breeders and veterinarians for good reason. In the wild, dogs instinctively look for small shelters or dens so they can safely sleep, nurse their babies, and recuperate. A crate is the modern-day version of that traditional den. It's a dog's personal safety space.

Crate training can help both with potty training and decreasing anxiety, especially when your dog is left alone. A smaller place helps your dog feel safer and more in control. It also helps your new Schnauzer adjust to your home until she learns your family's rules, including where she can or can't go potty.

However, leaving your dog alone all day in a crate, then crating again at night may be too much, making your Schnauzer feel anxious and alone. Also, the crate should never be used as a form of punishment, and you should never bang on the crate or yell at your Schnauzer while she's inside the crate. The crate needs to be a safe place for your dog, not one that she fears.

Choosing a Crate

Crates come in a variety of sizes and materials. Two key considerations are choosing a crate that is well ventilated and just big enough for your Schnauzer to be able to stand up and turn around inside. A crate that is too big will permit your dog to have an accident in an area other than her bedding, which can make potty training more difficult.

When choosing a crate for a puppy, keep in mind that your puppy will grow. If you purchase a crate based on the size your Schnauzer will grow to be, choose one that comes with a divider. This will allow you to make the crate snugger for your pup when she is small, and then you can expand the crate as she grows.

Put blankets or a bed in the bottom of the crate, along with some toys. Make sure they are hardy enough to not be chewed up by your new pup. Keep an eye out for any toy or bed that has been torn open and dispose of it. You can also cover the crate with a blanket to help create a den. Just be cautious of making it too hot inside.

Introducing Your Dog to the Crate

Crate training takes time, from a few days to a few weeks. For it to be effective, the crate should be associated with pleasant experiences, and you should take it slowly.

As discussed earlier, you should set up a crate for your new dog somewhere that she can easily access, especially if your Schnauzer needs a safe space to go and unwind.

Introduce your Schnauzer to her new crate by talking gently to her. Open the crate door and secure it so that it can't accidentally swing and hit your dog.

You can help coax your dog into her crate by putting a few pieces of food or treats near the crate door, then inside the crate. (If that doesn't work, you

Photo Courtesy
of Deborah Holmes

might try using a toy.) Be patient, and don't force your pup inside. It may take a little while.

Once your dog begins going into the crate, start keeping your Schnauzer there for small periods of time when you are home. You can create a command, like "go kennel" and point inside the crate with a treat in your hand, which you can give your dog—along with praise—after you shut the door.

Next, stay calmly near the crate for a few minutes, then leave your dog alone in the crate. Continue this procedure multiple times each day, gradually increasing the amount of time you leave your dog in the crate. After your new Schnauzer can last 30 minutes in the crate without becoming anxious when you are out of sight, you should be able to crate while you are gone for a short period of time.

*Photo Courtesy
of Suni Rae and Greg Miller*

Feeding in the Crate

If you start feeding your dog meals near the crate, your dog will have a positive association with the crate. Once you get your Schnauzer to go into the crate, place her food inside, near the back. If she is still hesitant to go inside, just place the food right in the door, then keep pushing the bowl slightly further towards the back at each mealtime. Close the door after your dog is comfortably in the crate. Begin by opening the door as soon as your dog has eaten, then extend the time slowly between feedings and door openings.

Whining in the Crate

If your dog begins to whine as you increase the time, go ahead and let her out at first. Slowly make her stay in longer; you don't want her to learn that whining is a way to get out of the crate.

If your dog whines while in the crate, she may need to use the bathroom, but she may also just be testing to see if you'll let her out. If she's just trying to get attention, she will likely stop after a couple of minutes. If your Schnauzer is still whining, say the term you use to indicate going outside to use the bathroom (e.g., "go potty"). If your dog gets excited, take her out of the crate and immediately lead her outside to use the bathroom.

Crating for Bedtime

You may want to place your dog's crate in or near your room at bedtime so your dog doesn't feel alone, especially at first. You might be able to move the crate farther away from you as your pup gets used to sleeping in it at night.

You may also want to practice crating your Schnauzer for naps during the day. Start slowly and work your way up to longer times.

Correcting Negative Behaviors

As perfect as your new pup may seem, all dogs misbehave from time to time. Again, it's important to establish rules and expectations from the very beginning, and to correct negative behavior early on.

While dog trainers implement a variety of strategies for training dogs, here are two things to keep in mind:

Dogs—and puppies in particular—have a lot of extra energy that they need to burn off. If you don't encourage them to do it positively, they will do it negatively through things like chewing, digging, and barking. You can help your Schnauzer burn off energy with activities like going for walks or playing fetch, tug-of-war, or using toys that dispense treats, like a Kong toy.

One of the best, most effective types of dog training is redirection, and it can be used to help with several unwanted behaviors. The technique involves getting your dog to stop unwanted behaviors by redirecting her focus on positive behavior. For example, if your dog starts chewing on something, such as a shoe, remove the shoe, say "no," then give the dog a chew toy. Be cautious of giving your dog items that are similar to what she is not supposed to chew, like an old shoe.

With these two methods in mind, let's look at some common bad behaviors you'll want to correct:

Chewing

Dog-proofing doesn't stop just because your puppy is now home with you, so don't slack off. Some of the things to consistently pay attention to are electrical cords, houseplants, medicine, small toys, etc.

It's also important to give your dog chew toys to help provide mental stimulation, keep teeth healthy, and reduce teething pain. Watch puppies closely when chewing, as their teeth may be able to puncture or bite off small pieces of items, which could cause a choking hazard or intestinal blockage. Choose chew toys wisely. Rubber chew toys that can be filled with a treat are good for keeping dogs occupied and safe. Rawhides and dental chews are also an option, but too many can be problematic and even cause intestinal blockages, so be careful when giving these and watch your pup closely.

Despite all your precautions, your new Schnauzer most likely will, at some point, still chew on something she's not supposed to. This is when redirection, as discussed above, can be used.

Another option to try is repellents, like Bitter Apple, designed to make items taste bad. You can usually find these online or at your local pet store.

Growling and Barking

Schnauzers are extremely protective of their families, and barking is one of their trademarks. We talked earlier about the need to socialize your dog from the start to help her become more used to being around other people and dogs, and in turn, reduce barking and growling.

When your Schnauzer barks or growls, interrupt her but don't punish. Again, redirecting is a good option. For example, if your dog starts to bark when you are walking, turn and go the other way. When your Schnauzer barks at home, you can spritz her with water from a spray bottle or shake a can filled with a few pennies near her as a distraction.

Schnauzers are naturally territorial and therefore see strangers as a possible threat to their family. While there's not one solution that works for everyone, the thing that works best for us is to take away our Schnauzer's "door privileges"—i.e., we leave the door open for her to look out, but we close it with a "no barking" command when she gets too out of control. She has started to growl more without a full-on bark in many situations now because she knows the consequence. (This does not always work, however.)

Here are some other things that do NOT work, according to the experts:

1. Don't yell, and especially don't ever hit your Schnauzer. When you yell, you make your dog more anxious. Additionally, from your dog's vantage point, your yelling may sound a lot like barking.
2. Don't muzzle your dog to prevent barking.
3. Don't use an anti-bark collar. Both muzzles and anti-bark collars can cause additional behavioral problems.

Here are some things you can do:

1. Obscure your dog's view so she can't see outside. In addition to blocking doors or windows so your dog can't see out of them, you can use a baby gate to keep your dog away from windows. A tall wooden fence is also a good outdoor option.

2. Distract your dog. A shake can or shaking keys might help. The sound startles your dog and distracts (i.e., redirects). After shaking the object, call your dog to you, tell her to sit, and give a treat if she sits and stops barking. (You can also use the "stay" command.)

3. Teach "quiet" by holding your Schnauzer's muzzle when she starts to bark. After a while, try "quiet" without holding her muzzle. This allows your dog to bark a few times, but she must stop when you say "quiet."

4. Give treats when your dog is about to bark on a walk. Again, this is a re-direction technique to distract.

Digging

Miniature Schnauzers, in particular, were bred as ratters, which means they had to dig in order to find and catch their prey. So digging is a natural instinct for many of these dogs. (My Schnauzer, however, is not a big digger except for burying bones or other treats like a piece of rock-hard pizza crust she once managed to sneak out of the garbage.)

As it is an ingrained instinct, it may be impossible to get your Schnauzer to completely stop digging, but there are some things you can do to help with the issue.

- **Give your Schnauzer attention and exercise** – As already mentioned, the more you can wear your dog out, the less likely she will be to partake in destructive behavior. The same goes for attention. Sometimes digging is a way of acting out in order to get your attention, even if it's negative attention.

- **Give a firm "No!"** – Just like any negative behavior, you have to catch your Schnauzer in the act for her to understand you are disapproving of an activity like digging. If you do catch your dog in the act, use a strong voice and say "NO!" (Again, it is never okay to hit your dog!)

- **Use a shaker can or spray bottle when you catch your dog digging.**

- **Block areas of frequent digging** – Use some form of barricade or partially bury big flat rocks or chicken wire in areas where your Schnauzer likes to dig.

- **Give your Schnauzer a safe place to dig** – You can set up a designated area—a sandbox of sorts—where it's okay for your pup to dig. Use garden beams to create the area, fill it with fresh soil, then bury smelly treats, etc., in the area. If you catch your dog digging in another area, give a firm "No digging!" then move your Schnauzer to the designated digging area.

Try the above tactics first. If they don't work, there are some tougher methods you can try.

- Put your dog's poop in the holes where she is digging. Note that this only works if your dog hates her feces; some dogs love to eat their own poop.
- Place citrus peels around the area where your Schnauzer is digging. Some dogs dislike the smell; for others, the odor is not a big deal
- Set up sprinklers near your dog's favorite digging ground and turn them on if you catch your dog digging. Sometimes sprinklers can be set up with motion sensors to turn on automatically when your dog gets too close.

If your dog is a digger, you need to take some special precautions to keep her from digging under your fence and escaping.

Line your fence with large rocks or bury chicken wire along the bottom of the fence. Also make sure your dog has a shaded, safe place to escape to during hot/cold weather or storms. Dogs will often try to escape their yards if the weather is too extreme.

Separation Anxiety

Schnauzers live for being with their families, and when their families are gone from home, they deeply feel the loss. Being left alone can be extremely stressful for them.

Dogs who struggle with separation anxiety often act out in unappealing ways, and it's a common reason why owners give up their dogs. Here are a few symptoms of a dog acting out due to separation anxiety:

- Using the bathroom indoors, even if housebroken
- Chewing and tearing things up
- Howling or whining excessively
- Pacing obsessively
- Attempting to escape.

All dogs may do a few of these things occasionally, but those with separation anxiety exhibit these behaviors consistently.

Separation anxiety is frustrating and can be destructive. Again, it's one of the top reasons people relinquish their dogs to animal shelters.

So what can you do?

- Don't make a big deal about leaving or coming home.
- Give your Schnauzer a special treat or toy only when you leave. Take it away when you get home.

Photo Courtesy of Candi Harringa

- Leave some form of clothing with your smell on it for your dog.
- Do the things you do before leaving—e.g., picking up keys or putting on shoes—at times other than when you leave to reduce the anxiety of your dog realizing certain actions mean you're heading out.
- Work up to leaving the house. Leave out the front door, just stand outside for a few seconds, then come back.
- Use a crate.

If you suspect your dog suffers from separation anxiety, talk to your veterinarian about suggestions.

Running Away

When we first moved to our house two years ago, we thought the yard was secure, but Puggles kept getting out somehow. (We finally figured out there was a spot next to the house where she could squeeze through the fence.) Our street is used as a cut-through by cars wanting to avoid traffic, and we also live perpendicular to a very busy road. Puggles getting out was terrifying!

No matter how well you think you've secured your yard, dogs can get out from time to time. Make sure you keep a collar on your dog with your contact information. Also, have your Schnauzer microchipped. A lot of times there are fundraisers where microchipping is offered at a significant discount. (We paid just $10 at such an event for Puggles!) If your Schnauzer gets out and is picked up, it is so much easier to find her if she has a tagged collar and is microchipped.

There are some other things you can do to help keep your Schnauzer from running away.

1. **Spay or neuter** – As I've mentioned, most shelter strays are unneutered males or females in heat, which indicates they probably got out of their yard and ran away. The inborn, physiological drive to breed is overwhelming for unneutered dogs, and if they sense a female in heat, they will most likely try to get to her. The same holds true for females in heat who will go try to find a mate.

2. **Upgrade your fencing** – A tall fence that your Schnauzer can't jump over is best, and generally considered more effective than an electric fence. Keep an eye out for things like rocks or fallen limbs that could help your dog climb over.

3. **Tire your dog out** – Again, keeping your Schnauzer active and busy helps with all kinds of problems, including getting out of the yard. A tired dog is more likely to be happy staying inside a fence.

4. **Train your Schnauzer before she gets out** – When your dog is running, teach her to quickly lie down and earn a treat. Then teach your Schnauzer not to go through a gate until a command is given. Finally, teach her to come to you when called.

Leaving Your Dog Alone at Home

We've discussed some of the things to consider before leaving your dog home alone for extended amounts of time, like keeping your home safe and using a crate. If you aren't going to use a crate, at least limit the amount of space where your dog will be allowed without supervision.

You should also create a routine for when you are preparing to leave your dog. Put your dog in the crate 15 minutes or so before you leave. Be matter-of-fact when getting ready to leave, give a short amount of praise, and give your dog a treat. Then when you get back home, stay calm, and even leave your dog in the crate for a short while. This will help prevent your Schnauzer from associating crating with being left alone.

Unfortunately, there's really no great way to leave your dog home alone for extended periods of time. If possible, come home during your lunch break to let your dog outside to use the bathroom or to go for a quick walk and let your Schnauzer burn off some energy. Or, you might consider hiring a dog walker.

HELPFUL TIP
Puppy Cam

As more and more options become available, many pet owners are choosing to install pet cameras to enable uninterrupted surveillance of pets who have been left at home. Some of these devices come with an app that's accessible via smartphone, and many come with two-way audio. Whether you're running a quick errand or you work away from home, a pet camera could ease your mind about how your dog is coping without you at home.

If you have a puppy, expect accidents. A basic rule of thumb is that a puppy can hold its urine one hour for every month of age. So, for example, a three-month-old puppy can go about three hours without having to go potty. If you're gone eight or more hours, you're going to come home to accidents. Training the puppy to use pee pads is a good option. However, a bored or stressed-out pup may tear those pads up or even ingest them.

Ideally, you will have a few days at home with your new Schnauzer before you need to leave her alone. During that time, you can slowly work your way up to leaving her for extended periods of time. Start small, just stepping outside for a few minutes and locking the door. (Listen to see how she responds.) Then slowly work up to a longer period of time.

When you leave your dog home alone, make sure that you provide for her needs: food, water, bedding, toys (be cautious, because your pup might choke if she tears the toy to bits), etc.

When you leave, make sure the temperature is comfortable for your dog and leave a light on. You can also add some background noise, like calming music or nature sounds, to help drown out any scary noises your Schnauzer may hear during the day.

Tiring your dog out before you leave is best. If possible, get up early and take your pup for a nice long walk or play fetch in the yard before you head out. That will help ease anxiety and reduce acting out.

When it's time to leave, stay calm and don't show your Schnauzer too much attention. You want to make leaving as laid-back as possible. As hard as it is, when you return home, stay calm and don't overindulge your pup. Too much attention feeds separation anxiety.

Finally, it's a good idea to have a friend or professional dog walker's contact information in case you run into problems getting home and need someone to check in on your dog.

CHAPTER 6
House-training Your Schnauzer

"Pay attention to your puppy, when they are looking around and smell-ing the floor that can be a good indication that they are trying to find their spot to potty. You need to pick them up and take them to where you want them to eliminate and use a key word like 'potty' so they can identify with the request."

RHONDA SMITH
Heavenly Miniature Schnauzer

House-training is one of the most important but often most frustrat-ing parts of training your new Schnauzer. The good news is that Schnauzers are very smart and are one of the easier dogs to house-train. Even older Schnauzers who have never been potty trained can quickly learn with consistency and praise.

The process of house-training both puppies and older dogs is the same, with the exception being that older dogs can wait longer between bathroom visits.

Different House-training Options

HELPFUL TIP
Eco-Friendly
House-training

Accidents happen, especially when you're teaching a new puppy where (and where not) to do its business. Puppy pads are a convenient and easy way to control the damage done to your home during the house-training process. An eco-friendly alternative to disposable puppy pads is reusable puppy pads that can be washed after being soiled and then reused. Check your local and online pet supply stores for options.

When it comes to house-training your Schnauzer, you have a few possibilities of how to go about it, largely depending on your availability.

1. Crate Training – As we've talked about in other chap-ters, a crate is a great option for puppies and older dogs alike. Again, the crate needs to be just big enough for your puppy to be able to stand up and turn around in. If it's too big, your Schnauzer will use it as a bathroom. With a small

Photo Courtesy of Ann Schuh

crate, however, your dog is not going to want to soil her bedding and will wait as long as possible to go potty.

If you're not available to take your puppy outside during the day, and you can't get someone to come to do it for you, crate training is not your best option for potty training during the day, especially for a puppy.

2. **Puppy Pads** – If you're going to be gone several hours during the day, a better solution is placing your puppy in a small, safely confined area—such as a puppy playpen—with puppy pads. You can place your dog's crate in the area so she has a safe place to sleep, but leave the crate door open so your Schnauzer can use the bathroom outside the crate.

When setting up your Schnauzer's confined area, place puppy pads as far away from your dog's bed (or crate) as possible. Your Schnauzer will naturally want to avoid going potty near her bed.

Puppy pads also provide a good option when the weather is too bad to go outside, when you are asleep, or when you just can't get to the door in time.

3. **Outdoor Training** – Even if you are crate training or using puppy pads, you ideally want your puppy to learn to go outside. Making this happen quickly and effectively depends on you.

There are several times a day when you will need to take your Schnauzer outside. Note that I said "take" your dog outside, not "send" your dog outside. It initially has to be a team effort between you and your dog. You need to go out with your Schnauzer every time she goes outside until your dog is completely housebroken so that you can reward your pup for her hard work.

The First Few Weeks

"Be very attentive to when the puppy wakes up from a nap, most every time they will be ready to go potty as soon as they are awake."

TIMOTHY SWAIN
Swains Sweet Schnauzers

House-training your Schnauzer is not that difficult, but it does require a little time and a lot of commitment to be successful. If you are home with your dog and consistently train her, your puppy (or older untrained dog) can be potty trained in as little as one to two weeks. If you leave your dog alone for several hours a day, it may take more like a month or two for your Schnauzer to become completely housebroken.

Puppies cannot be potty trained until they are old enough to go on their own. For the first three or four weeks of life, puppies don't naturally know how to eliminate their waste. To get those bodily functions working properly, the mother dog must lick and groom her pups to stimulate them to pee or poop, usually right after feeding.

Photo Courtesy of Kaycie Vidrine PhotographybyKV

PHOTOGRAPHY BY KV

Once puppies learn to go without their mother's help, the official potty-training process can begin. The greater your commitment, the faster and more successful potty training your Schnauzer will be.

Up until about six months, a good rule of thumb is that however many months old a puppy is, that's about the maximum number of hours she can wait before using the bathroom. So, for example, a four-month-old pup needs to use the bathroom about once every four hours.

Additionally, puppies usually need to go potty after they eat, so when she finishes a meal, you should always take your Schnauzer outside. It's also important to take your pup outside after naps, exercise, when you first wake up, and right before bed.

"Be consistent with all training. Feed at a set time; take the pup out after eating. Put the pup to bed at the same time, and get up at the same time to take the pup out," adds Pat A. Hunt of Alpats Miniature Schnauzers.

Make sure you take your dog outside using the same door every time. Additionally, come up with a consistent term, like "go potty," and say it when your dog starts to do her business.

Until your dog is potty trained, you may want to take her out on a leash, even if you have a fenced yard. This way you can consistently take your dog

Photo Courtesy of Dana Stettin

to the same spot or area of the yard to defecate. If you do this consistently, your Schnauzer will soon know this is the area where she should go potty.

Finally, watch for your dog's warning signs. My Schnauzer will stand by the back door when she's ready to go out, but she's recently had a couple of accidents in the middle of the night because I confused her "need to go potty" routine with her "there's a raccoon in the backyard I want to go bark at" routine and ignored her. If your dog is sniffing around, whining, turning circles, etc., she may be hinting she needs to go.

Crate Training

"Crate training! Keep your puppy confined to one area of the home until fully trained (this is a must). Always use a key word such as 'out' when taking them outside. Always use the same door and same area outside. Praise them and give them a treat when they successfully go potty. Ideally set up a small pen area and take puppy there so they can't run around the yard. Once successful, praise, treat, and then they can be let out into the yard. This will keep their attention in the task at hand."

BARBARA DURRANCE
Show Stopper Schnauzers

Leaving your Schnauzer in her crate all day is never ideal, but especially when it comes to house-training. Young puppies simply cannot hold off on using the bathroom that long. Remember the months-old to hours-she-can-hold ratio I mentioned earlier.

If you choose to use a crate, make sure you immediately take your dog outside to potty as soon as you let her out. It doesn't matter if your Schnauzer has been in the crate five minutes or five hours—take her outside when she leaves the crate.

As mentioned in a previous chapter, your dog may whine while in the crate at night, which could be a sign she needs to go out, or it could be a sign she wants attention. At first, it's best to go ahead and take your Schnauzer out. With time, you will hopefully learn to differentiate between your dog's cries.

After your dog goes potty, let her run around the yard for a minute. Don't put her back in the crate immediately. Otherwise, you're teaching your Schnauzer that playtime ends as soon as she goes potty, so she will put off going.

Using Doggy Doors and Playpens

Some people like to use a doggy door so their Schnauzer can go outside on its own. For the safety of your dog as well as your property, it's best not to allow your dog to roam the entire house or yard alone until she can do so without issue. Also, a doggy door will not help with house-training until your dog knows to go outside to potty. However, once those basics are understood, a doggy door can be a great option since your Schnauzer will not be reliant on you to let her out when nature calls.

We already talked about the need for setting up a confined space for your dog. You can do this with your doggy door, as well as by setting up a dog playpen or baby gate so your Schnauzer can go outside through the doggy door but will not have access to the rest of the house.

Dogs often don't like crawling through tight spaces, so you will have to train your Schnauzer to use the doggy door. Once the area is set up, place your dog in the confined area and step just outside the doggy door. Call your Schnauzer by name, and hold treats to encourage her to come through. If your dog acts afraid of the door's swinging motion, you may need to tape the door so it stays open until she gets used to using it. Keep practicing this routine from both sides of the doggy door until your Schnauzer learns to walk through on her own. Then guide your dog to where you want her to go potty and praise her for doing well. With time and consistency, your Schnauzer will learn to go potty outside on her own using the doggy door.

Photo Courtesy of Anttu Suhonen

Dealing with Accidents

While potty training, accidents will happen.

When your dog has an accident, clean it up using a rag or paper towel as quickly as possible. Follow up with a carpet-cleaning product and an odor neutralizer. Next, use vinegar or a dog repellent spray to keep your dog from going again in that same spot.

Sometimes even house-trained dogs will have accidents. If your potty-trained dog starts going where she's not supposed to when you're gone, it could be due to separation anxiety. It could also be due to a health issue, such as a urinary tract infection, so it's wise to have your housebroken dog checked out by your vet if her potty habits suddenly change.

Some dogs also cannot hold their urine when they are excited. Your best bet in these situations is to not pay attention to them right when you get home. Other dogs will pee a little as an act of submission when they first see you. Remember, they can't help it, and scolding will not make things better. Talk to your vet or a dog trainer for suggestions on how to help the situation, especially if your dog is acting out of submission.

Always Reward, Never Punish.

Punishing your pup for accidents by rubbing her nose in it, or worse, is not only unkind; it probably won't work. Puppies must make the connection between their actions—i.e., going potty—and your immediate reaction. Also, you should never strike your pup—potty training or otherwise.

If you catch your Schnauzer going potty inside, give a calm but firm "No!", then immediately take her outside.

Dogs want to please their humans, and a heartfelt "good boy" (or girl) along with some extra pets or cuddles is a great reward. Doing this every time you see your pup successfully go potty outside or on a pad is imperative.

Potty training your Schnauzer is not a complex process, but your dedication is essential to success. The more committed you are to the process, the sooner you'll see results, and the happier both you and your Schnauzer will be.

CHAPTER 7
Socializing with People and Animals

"Once they have all their vaccinations, take the puppy everywhere allowed! In the meantime have friends and family over with everyone handling and playing with the puppy. Schnauzers are people dogs so they socialize very easily."

BARBARA DURRANCE
Show Stopper Schnauzers

S ocializing refers to helping your Schnauzer adjust to new people, new animals, new places, and new experiences. The more socialized your dog is, the happier and healthier she'll be. It will also make life easier for both you and your Schnauzer. Here's how:

- Socialized dogs experience less anxiety and fear. Dogs who are fearful are more likely to bark, growl, and even bite. They also are more likely to run away.

- Socialized dogs do better at the groomer, going to the veterinarian, etc.

- Socialized dogs are better at traveling. Whether it's a car trip across town or across country, it's no fun having a dog that is super hyper in the car.

Photo Courtesy
of Dagne Sereicikiene

Photo Courtesy of Louize Carpio

(Trust me, I know!) Taking your Schnauzer on practice car rides often can help reduce her anxiety in a moving vehicle.

- Socialized dogs get more exercise. You can't take an aggressive dog to the dog park. It's also easier to take dogs on walks when they are well socialized.

Introducing Your Dog to New People

"On socializing I always suggest that you take your puppy with you to any businesses where they are allowed, like building supply stores and pet supply stores. And introduce them to children every chance you get, as this will keep them social. It's always a good idea to ask people to pet your puppy so they will accept different people."

RHONDA SMITH
Heavenly Miniature Schnauzer

One of the easiest ways to help your dog get used to being around other people is to take her for regular walks in an area where you will run across other people. Ideally, you want a well-used route where individuals of all shapes and sizes—big, small, male, female, and children—hang out. The more diverse the area, the sounds, the sights, and the people, the better.

Taking your dog for regular walks will help her feel more comfortable and confident with the world around her. However, it can take time for a dog to get comfortable being around other people, pets, and places. It's important to pay attention to your dog's body language, especially watching out for signs of anxiety. These can include things like tail tucked between the legs, ears flattened back, yawning, nose or lip licking, as well as more obvious signs like shaking, whining, and hair standing on end.

When it comes to socializing your dog, go at your dog's pace—especially if your Schnauzer is a rescue and you aren't familiar with her background. Pushing your dog too far too quickly will likely cause negative associations with the experience, and you want socialization to be positive.

When new people approach, there are a few key elements to keep in mind. First, remain calm. Your dog will sense if you are nervous and will imitate your behavior. You may want to carry treats to use as positive reinforcement when your dog meets new people. However, if your dog is meeting other dogs, the treats can become a problem and might actually start a dog fight.

Before people reach out to pet your dog, give them some instructions. Make sure they keep their hands where the dog can see them and pet from underneath, like on the chin. If your dog acts skittish but not really aggressive, try to make the experience positive by starting off with brief introductions. Once your Schnauzer gets stressed, the experience becomes negative, and your dog will not learn. That's why it's important to start small. If you want your dog to be able to go down a busy street, for example, start on a quiet street and work your way up. Offer tons of praise and encouragement.

Photo Courtesy of Abigail Colbert

Introducing Your Dog to Children

Children love dogs, and dogs often love children—but it can also be a dangerous mix. Kids are small and loud and often not as cautious as they should be when meeting a new dog, and that can be scary for your Schnauzer. If a young, unfamiliar child wants to pet your dog, it's up to you to use caution as to whether or not you allow it.

Before you let any young child pet your Schnauzer, your dog should know some basic commands like "sit" and "down." Also, if you know your dog is going to be meeting children, you may

Photo Courtesy of Priscilla Boles

want to practice petting your dog more like an untrained child would—stroking a little harder, gently playing with her tail, etc. Get on your knees while doing this, so that you are shorter. Then be sure to give plenty of praise and treats.

Meeting Other Dogs

It's best to begin socializing with other dogs while they are both on a leash. That way you maintain control of the situation if things head south.

Ideally, you don't want to let your dog and the new dog sniff each other first. A better option is to take them on a walk together, single file. This lets them get used to the idea of being around each other and wearing off a little bit of energy in the process.

If you meet another dog walker along your outing, try to keep moving past each other. Stay positive and praise your dog. You need to stay relaxed, and praising is a good way to do that. Even if your Schnauzer barks, keep moving forward. Don't freak out. If the dogs stop and sniff each other, try to stay calm and aware of your dog's body language, as well as that of the other dog's. Then, keep moving.

Before you let your dog run loose at a dog park, make sure your Schnauzer knows the command "come." This will help significantly if a scary situation arises. It's also important should your dog somehow escape the fenced area so that she doesn't run off.

For Miniature Schnauzers, try to find a dog park that has a small dog section to minimize the risk of injury. For your first dog park outings, you

STORY
Miniature Therapy Dog

In 2015, a Miniature Schnauzer named Bella spent 296 hours visiting patients in a local hospital in Delaware. A rescue dog from the Kent County SPCA shelter, Bella passed the American Kennel Club Canine Good Citizen class and later began volunteering with her owner at Bayhealth Kent General Hospital in Dover, as well as various nursing homes. Bella has earned the AKC Distinguished Therapy Dog for her 400 visits to help others.

may not want to actually take your dog into the park but rather walk near and around the park. Let your dog go up to the outer fence and see how she responds when unknown dogs come running over. (Remember to offer praise. Don't bring your dog's toys or treats to the dog park. This can create problems and fights with other dogs.) If your Schnauzer acts aggressively, back away from the fence, but don't leave. Slowly work your way closer (this may need to happen on multiple trips).

When you are ready to let your dog try running off-leash in the park, pick a time when the park is less likely to be crowded. Weekends and evenings are usually the busiest times, especially when the weather is nice.

Take off your dog's leash when you enter the park. It may seem scary, but keeping the leash on can cause your dog to become more stressed, and it can injure her if she gets tangled up. And, if you act nervous and keep holding your dog on a leash, she will sense your nervousness and will become more anxious.

Stay back and watch your dog interact with the other dogs. If another dog snaps at your Schnauzer, try not to react. Your dog will learn. Calling your dog over (e.g., "Puggles, come!") will help reassure her that you are still in control; she is safe; you want her to have fun; and you are there if she needs you. If you sense your dog is not having fun, it's time to leave.

Socializing Your Schnauzer with Other Pets

Puggles was my children's first pet, but she was far from the last. We currently have two cats—one that is very timid (Poppy) and one that is fearless (Boo). Puggles and Boo are best friends. Puggles loves to wrestle—something she learned from a Yorkie at the local dog park—and she and Boo are wrestling buddies. It amazes me how gentle Puggles is with Boo when they play.

We also had two guinea pigs that Puggles loved. She knew not to bother them, but would give them kisses if I held them. Same thing with a rabbit.

What's funny to me, however, is that while she is super gentle with our pets, Puggles will chase—and occasionally even kill—animals (including rabbits) that are out in the yard and not part of our family. She goes ballistic when a neighbor's cat crosses into our yard. As a Schnauzer, her number one job is to "protect" her family, and she seems to know that our other pets are included in family; the neighbors' cats or wild bunnies are not.

We foster animals through the local shelter somewhat regularly, and introducing Puggles to new pets is always a little stressful. Although we haven't had a bad episode, we just never know how the other animal is going to respond.

Here are some tips to help with socializing your Schnauzer with your other non-canine pets.

1. Take your dog for a walk before you introduce other pets. You want her to get as much extra energy out as possible before the introduction.

2. One way that animals communicate with each other is by using pheromones, a chemical produced by animals of the same species. There are some commercially available pheromones designed to help both dogs or cats feel relaxed, which can help with the introduction.

3. Put your Schnauzer on a leash, then allow both of your pets to be in the same room, keeping a good grasp on the leash.

4. If you're introducing a cat, allow the cat to roam free while your Schnauzer is still on a leash. Stay this way until both animals are calm. (This may take a few introductions.) Until both animals seem calm around each other, keep them separated or keep your Schnauzer on a leash around the cat. Always keep the animals separated when you aren't home until they are calm around each other.

5. Use praise, treats, and other rewards when your Schnauzer does something good around the other pet. Playtime might not be the best option because it can cause excitement, and you want your dog to be calm during the introduction.

6. When it comes to introducing caged pets (like a guinea pig, for example,) make sure your dog knows "sit" and "down," and ideally, "stay" and "come." With someone holding your dog on a leash, have her sit (and ideally, "stay," at a distance), and hold your other pet high enough where your dog can see it but not reach it. If your dog stays calm, lower the other pet so she can sniff. Reward your Schnauzer for doing a good job.

A Final Note

Remember that socialization is a process. It takes time, patience, and consistency. However, the more socialized your Schnauzer is, the better the experience will be for both your family and your new dog.

CHAPTER 8
Establishing Your Pack

Dogs are believed to have descended from wolves, and as such, still have the "pack mentality" of their ancestors. In the wild, wolves have a social hierarchy of roles, which is governed by each wolf's position in the pack. The leader is known as the alpha, and can be a male or a female. In your home, that alpha needs to be human.

When bringing a new dog into the household, you—i.e., the humans—need to become the leaders, although one human will become the alpha. If you have multiple dogs, one dog will be the dog leader, but a human should still be the pack alpha, and all humans—even young children—need to be seen as having a higher rank in the pack.

Dogs learn early on from their mothers that there are rules and consequences. This makes it easier to teach your new Schnauzer the rules of the house. Just remember that when it comes to humans, dogs do much better with positive reinforcement like praise and treats.

Photo Courtesy
of LisaDawn McCabe

From the moment you get your new Schnauzer, you must begin establishing yourself as the leader of the pack. Here are some ways to do that:

1. **Communicate with energy and emotion** – Dogs communicate primarily nonverbally. When your dog does something good, your own nonverbal communication needs to express that clearly to your dog. When your dog does something bad, again, your nonverbal behavior needs to express that but NEVER by hitting or screaming. Be firm, confident, and assertive, but not abusive.

2. **Teach commands like "come, "sit," and "down," among others** – This training begins by using treats, but if your dog doesn't eventually learn to obey without treats, you may not be seen as the alpha.

3. **Teach your dog to walk politely next to you** – (I admit I have failed at this one.) To be the leader, you have to be in charge of everything on your walks. No tugging. No marking territory without your permission. And especially no barking or bad behavior towards other humans or animals.

4. **Feed your dog on *your* schedule, not hers** – In the wild, some wolves lower down in the pecking order don't get to eat for weeks, even if they helped with the hunt. The alpha also controls who gets to drink. You should never keep water or food from your dog, but controlling feeding times helps establish you as the alpha.

5. **Define where your dog is and isn't allowed in the house** – Does your dog have free range of the house? Does she get to sleep on your bed? These are your choices as the leader, and the more rules you set, the easier it is to become the alpha.

6. **Come and go without permission** – Strong leaders help keep the rest of the pack from feeling anxious, even when the alpha is gone. When the alpha leaves, the rest of the pack patiently and confidently waits for his return. As the leader, you should avoid turning leaving the house into a big deal. Just a short "be good" to your dog, or something along those lines is enough. Same goes for when you get home. Don't make returning home a big deal, and don't show your dog a lot of attention until she calms down—especially if you're dealing with separation anxiety issues.

7. **Be consistent** – Changing the rules or making exceptions will only confuse your dog. It can't be okay for your dog to get on the furniture one day but not on the next. Dogs need consistency and repetition in order to understand the rules.

8. **Offer affection** – Dogs do better when they receive encouragement and affection. Praise your dog for jobs well done. Play together. Cuddle together. Help your dog feel she is an important member of your pack.

Raising Siblings

When picking out a Schnauzer puppy, it's easy to fall in love with more than one dog in a litter. Plus dogs are pack animals, so two pups from the same litter are better than one, right? Not according to the experts. In fact, some breeders won't even sell two littermates to the same family.

Any time you have two littermates together, there is a risk of "littermate syndrome," which leads to excessive fearfulness of humans and other animals. Here's why. Littermates tend to develop an incredibly strong bond, which can be detrimental because it causes incessant anxiety when the two pups are separated, even if only for a few minutes. Besides being unhealthy, it can also get in the way of basic obedience training.

The biggest problem is that puppies from the same litter already share a bond, which means that they may feel better being just the two of them as opposed to with the rest of the family. Their pack is already established. That bond makes it difficult for them each to become "whole," relying too much on the other sibling for their happiness. It also can make it hard for the dogs to open up to owners as part of their pack.

Additionally, the puppies are often too busy playing with each other to pay attention to their owner's commands. And again, they are so attached to each other that they cannot be separated from their sibling long enough to undergo one-on-one training with their owner.

Littermates also tend to fight with each other more than they would with dogs from other litters. This can be particularly problematic if you try to introduce a third dog into the mix.

Remember that purchasing a puppy is only the first of many expenses you will have over the years. Two dogs are twice the expense. In addition to twice the food, you're going to have twice the vet bills.

That's not to say having two littermates is all bad. For one, the dogs will have a playmate, which puts less responsibility on you. They can keep each other entertained and wear each other out.

They also learn how to bite softly because they correct each other when one bites too hard. Puggles is an expert at giving soft bites when she wrestles with my husband or our cat Boo. She will take Boo's entire head in her mouth but never hurts her.

If you are determined to get two littermates, your best bet is to separate them for significant lengths of time, starting as soon as possible after bringing them home. Feed, walk, train, and even crate them separately. They each need to learn how to function without having the other sibling around, and how to be content when they are alone. This is much more time-consuming and exhausting, but it's imperative for their well-being, especially after one of the siblings dies.

*Photo Courtesy
of Sarah LaGrone*

Photo Courtesy of Shaunda McKillip

Introducing Your Schnauzer to Your Other Dogs

If you already have a dog, you will have ideally introduced your dog to your new Schnauzer before making the decision to bring the Schnauzer home. But I realize that's not always possible, and it's sometimes hard to tell how the dogs will respond to another dog in their home territory.

At the shelter, we always recommend people bring their other dogs to meet the dog they are thinking of adopting. We take both dogs out to the backyard and keep them on a tight leash so they can sniff each other while we still have them under control. If things seem to go okay, we may take them off the leash and observe. If one dog is markedly smaller than the other(s), that one may come off first so that we still have control over the bigger dog(s) if things turn south.

Do not hold your dog while introducing her to other dogs. That can make the other dogs more anxious and/or aggressive. Also, stay calm during the introduction. Dogs can sense your anxiety, and it will make them anxious as well.

Discouraging Fighting and Other Negative Behaviors

If your new Schnauzer is a puppy, in particular, you're likely to experience some negative behavior in the way she responds to her family and other pets. Older dogs who have not been properly trained may have similar issues.

Fighting – If you already have a dog at home, there's a decent chance at some point your dog and your new Schnauzer will fight. This is normal, and may occur for a whole host of reasons. Hopefully the fight will be quick and minor. But if a bigger fight breaks out, be prepared.

Never get in the middle of the two dogs or attempt to grab them by the collar. You are almost guaranteed to get bitten. Get your kids out of the way so they don't get hurt. Stay as calm as possible and find a way to distract them by using the following ideas:

- Spray fighting dogs with a hose or water bottle if possible. (A bucket or even a cup of water may work if that's all you have.) Aim for the eyes and nose of the more aggressive dog.
- Make loud, jarring noises. An air horn or a slamming door are good options. You want something that will snap the dogs out of it. However, screaming and shouting often make things worse.

- Find an object to break up the fight. A blanket can be used to throw over the dogs and break their focus. Umbrellas (if the handles are long enough) or brooms can also be placed between the two dogs.
- Heavier objects, like chairs or laundry baskets, can be used to help separate the dogs.

Again, using your body to intervene is not recommended, and never, ever try to get in between two fighting dogs.

Nipping – Puppies use their mouths to play with each other, which is why they "bite" when they are playing or being petted. It's not intended to be aggressive. It's just how they operate. While it's somewhat tolerable when puppies are little, it's not so cute if they continue the behavior as they get older and bigger. And it's really not cute to your older dog if you have one.

Biting is ingrained in a puppy's nature, so you need to give your Schnauzer an alternative by redirecting her to a better chewing option like a chew toy.

You also need to teach your puppy to be gentle with hands or with your older dogs. (Your older dog will hopefully teach your puppy with a quick snap.) When your puppy nips at you, look at her directly and yell "OW!", then ignore her. You may even want to leave the room. Once she's calmed down, use the chew toy again.

Another way to discourage nipping is to loosely and gently hold your Schnauzer's jaw with your thumb and forefinger and not let go until she calms down. Wait several seconds, then release her jaw and offer your hand again. Praise her if she licks or ignores your hand. If she nips again, hold her jaw again and repeat the process.

You should never hit your Schnauzer for nipping. This can cause your dog to become afraid of you and/or of your hands. She may also get defensive and try to bite you. Finally, she may think you are playing and nip harder, thinking it's a game.

What if Your Dogs Don't Get Along?

When we first started taking Puggles to the dog park, one of the hardest things for me was when other less-friendly dogs would snap at her. She even got in a couple of scuffles with other dogs (they always attacked first). Just like she was learning to socialize, I was learning as well. When it came to the owners of grumpy, snappy dogs, they'd often say something along the lines of "let them be. She'll learn." And Puggles did.

Sometimes it's hard to tell if your dogs are playing or fighting. If one of your dogs is trying to get away and the other keeps pinning the dog down, then it's fighting—or at least it's not really play. When animals are playing, there are regular breaks in the action. This lets the animals catch their breath and calm down. Puggles also often sneezes, which is a signal that she is just playing. When done correctly, your dog will bow down in order to ask the other animal if she wants to play.

FUN FACT
GSCA

The Giant Schnauzer Club of America (GSCA) was founded in 1962. This non-profit club maintains a list of breeders, conducts dog shows, and works to protect the welfare of the breed. The American Kennel Club is the parent organization of the GSCA. Information about becoming a member of this club can be found at www.giantschnauzer-clubofamerica.com

Are the dogs using play body language? I already mentioned the play bow. Another common sign is when your dog "slaps" the ground with her front paws. Your dog may slap with her paws, lower her upper body, stick her rear end up in the air, then wait—sometimes while barking. Your dog may also start to run, hoping her playmate will follow suit.

A little bit of conflict is not unusual or necessarily harmful. Your dogs are establishing a pecking order. However, if issues don't work themselves out quickly or if you are fearful for any of your pets' safety, your best bet is to consult a professional trainer. Part of dog training involves teaching impulse control, which helps your dog stay calm instead of negatively responding to stimuli.

There are occasionally dogs that just do not do well with other animals. We had a wonderful, huge black lab at the shelter who was as sweet as could be until he got around other dogs. Taking him outside on a leash was a nightmare because not only was he super strong, but he was also super aggressive. He would bark and growl at every dog cage we passed, including puppies. In his case, the shelter insisted he only go to a single-pet home.

Introducing Your Schnauzer to Your Cats

Introducing Puggles and the cats was much more stressful for me. As I've mentioned before, we have two cats: Poppy and Boo. They are polar opposites. Poppy is the definition of a "fraidy cat," whereas Boo is fearless. They both like Puggles, though, because she knows how to properly respond to each. When Poppy gets scared, she hisses, and Puggles backs off. Boo, on the other hand, never hisses. It's always game on with her!

We have fostered a few dogs, however, who did not know how to get along with our cats. Poppy generally would just run, hide, hiss, and growl when these strange dogs entered our home. Boo, on the other hand, would try to play. One puppy literally dragged Boo down the stairs by her head. Boo squealed like it hurt but then jumped on the puppy to play some more. We also fostered a German Shepherd who completely ignored our cats. It really just depends on the dog.

Photo Courtesy
of Merry Morrissy-Karp

That said, Schnauzers—especially miniatures and puppies—are known for being active and hyper. Most likely, they are going to want to at least play with your cat. So, when first introducing your Schnauzer to your cat, keep the dog on a leash. There's a good chance your cat will just run off, and that's okay. Your cat needs to have dog-proof spots that serve as a safe haven. (Our home also has Boo-proof spots for Poppy!)

For the first few introductions, supervise carefully until you feel completely certain that your cat is going to be safe. I have a friend who recently got a tiny kitten, then her son accidentally left the door to the cat's safe haven open. A puppy got hold of her, and it ended tragically.

If things start to turn south, don't yell at or hit your pets. This adds tension to an already difficult situation, and your pets may misinterpret your yelling as confirming the other pet is indeed the enemy. Separate them as quickly and calmly as possible.

If things do not get better, call in a trainer.

What About Smaller Animals?

Remember that Schnauzers were originally bred to hunt rodents, so sometimes introducing your smaller furry pets to your dog is not a great idea. We've been lucky. Puggles was naturally able to determine the difference between pets and wild animals. She would give our guinea pigs kisses, but she's killed a few rats and rabbits in the yard over the years. She will cuddle up with our cats, but she goes ballistic if a strange cat enters our yard.

Your safest bet is to keep smaller rodents in locations that your Schnauzer can't reach. If you really want to introduce them, hopefully your Schnauzer has learned commands like "stay" and "come," then make your dog "stay" while you hold the pet, then ask her to "come" on your command. Otherwise, you should keep your dog on a leash while you let her sniff your pet. Watch your dog's body language. Keep interactions short and controlled, and repeat this step several times.

CHAPTER 9
Physical and Mental Exercise

Back in Chapter 1, we talked about the history of the Schnauzer. As a quick reminder, Standard Schnauzers were the original Schnauzer breed and were bred to help protect farms from vermin, herd farm animals, and protect their families. The miniature Schnauzer came on the scene a few centuries later and was designed to be a small farm dog that loved to hunt rodents. Giant Schnauzers started out in the Bavarian Alps as cattle dogs, as well as guard dogs.

No matter which type of Schnauzer you have, all were originally intended to be both physically and mentally active. Today's Schnauzers are typically selected to simply be pets, but their need for physical and mental exercise is still ingrained in their nature.

Photo Courtesy of Jason Hamm

Options for Physical Exercise

"Most Miniature Schnauzers need to be exercised a couple times a day. A brisk walk is good but playing a game of fetch in the yard is even better. They need their energy drained or they may begin to drain it themselves by chewing things or acting out."

PAT A. HUNT
Alpats Miniature Schnauzers

Schnauzers typically need to have at least 60 minutes of physical exercise a day, ideally something that will burn off a lot of energy in a short amount of time. This helps them to settle down and stay out of trouble.

One of the best ways to help your Schnauzer burn off energy is by taking a walk. This not only lets your dog get needed exercise, but it can help with mental stimulation. Plus it provides that all-important family bonding the breed craves.

Walks can be either be a single hour-long-walk, or broken up into two 30-minute outings. With Puggles, we have a nice three-mile route from our house to a local trail, then back home. She is older, and by the time we get home, she is happy and exhausted.

In my situation, I admit I have not done a good job of training Puggles to stay calm when it's walk time. She has learned that if I start looking for my yoga pants and/or tennis shoes, it's time for a walk—at least in her mind. (This became really problematic when I joined a gym!) If she sees me pull out headphones or a water bottle, she gets super excited to the point that it's loud and annoying.

Puggles' reaction is based on the fact that dogs like routine. It's best to walk your dog consistently at particular times of the day. I have also found that Puggles knows our normal route, and if I try to deviate because it's super hot outside, I need to cut it short for time, or I'm just not feeling up to three miles, she does not

FUN FACT
Lure Coursing

Giant Schnauzers are known for their agility and intelligence. One of the sports in which Giant Schnauzers are known to be adept is lure coursing. Lure coursing is a sport for dogs in which the canines pursue a mechanical lure. This is an opportunity for sighthound breeds to do what comes naturally in a safe and controlled environment.

accept the change well and is not satisfied when we get home. If we do our normal route, however, she is content and calm.

Walks are not the only way to help Schnauzers get their daily dose of exercise. Here are some other suggestions:

- **Trips to the Dog Park** – When Puggles was younger, we frequented our local dog park a lot. It was a great way to burn off energy, as well as gain that ever-important socialization. (She's a little less patient with other dogs now that she's 11.) An hour or so at the dog park, and she was ready to sleep when we got home, although she often needed a bath first.

- **Games** – Some Schnauzers like to play fetch with a ball or a Frisbee, which is another great form of exercise. If I try this with Puggles, she just watches the ball roll, then goes off and does something else. Fetch is definitely not a universal favorite with Schnauzers. It all depends on the dog. Chase can be a popular option with some Schnauzers.

- **Dog Toys** – Again, it's going to depend on the dog, but toys can also be a good option for some Schnauzers. With the exception of an occasional rope or sock for tug-of-war, Puggles has no interest in balls, stuffed animals, or other dog toys—but a lot of Schnauzers do.

- **Wrestling** – Besides walks, this is Puggles' favorite form of exercise, and it's something she learned early on from her friend Jack the Yorkie at the dog park. Before we got my cat, Boo, my husband was Puggles'

Photo Courtesy of Anttu Suhonen

wrestling buddy. He got down on all fours and gently "attacked" her head and body with his hand, as she jumped and gave "love bites" back, sometimes flipping over while Mike gently pushed her around. Now, she and Boo do this several times a day. (Boo keeps our Schnauzer young.)

- **"Hunting"** – Finally, if you have a fenced yard, another way to encourage a little extra exercise is to hang bird and squirrel feeders to attract wildlife. Remember, Miniature Schnauzers were designed to hunt these critters, and there's often nothing more exciting for them than a chance to chase. Just be mentally prepared for the fact that they may catch and kill small animals at times.

Options for Mental Exercise

Schnauzers are smart dogs by nature, and they need to be challenged mentally as well as physically.

One option for this is agility training. Dog agility training refers to directing your dog through a number of obstacles—like through tunnels, around poles, over teeter-totters, through hoops, and so on. While agility is an actual sport with competitions, any dog can learn some basic agility moves to stimulate them both physically and mentally.

Agility training plays into a Schnauzer's natural hunting instincts and skills, which involves running and weaving through barriers while chasing prey. While you can hire a professional for this undertaking, there are now inexpensive agility training kits available, and plenty of YouTube videos and other materials to teach you how to do this.

Agility courses also are a great way for your dog to continue to bond with you, the handler. Your Schnauzer has to learn to follow your verbal and hand cues to be able to properly navigate through the course. This strengthens your bond, and increases your dog's trust in you, plus it helps improve your dog's overall behavior.

While agility training is an excellent option for both physical and mental exercise, it does take time and commitment.

There are other ways you can work to keep your Schnauzer mentally stimulated as well. Here are some ideas:

1. **Continue teaching tricks** – We've talked about the need to teach your dog basic commands like sit and stay. But there are a lot of additional tricks that go beyond your basic commands. The more tricks your dog learns, the more confident he'll be. Again, find books or videos to help give you ideas and insights on how to properly train your dog.

2. **Make your Schnauzer work for her treats** – While it's easy to just set your Schnauzer's treats down, you can add mental stimulation by turning treat time into a game. For example, using a toy like a Kong (where you place the treat inside and your dog has to work to get it out) is a great way to keep your dog mentally stimulated, as well as out of trouble for a while.

3. **Invest in puzzle toys** – I already mentioned Kong toys, which are a type of puzzle toys, but there are plenty of other options out there. These typically are treat-dispensing toys that help your dog stay focused on a task for an extended length of time. Again, this kind of practice boosts confidence and improves overall behavior.

If you don't know how your dog will respond to such toys, or if you are on a budget, you can make your own. One example is to place a few treats in the cups of a muffin tin, then cover the treats with tennis balls (which should fit nicely into the muffin cups). Then let your dog work on getting the balls out and finding the treats.

4. **Teach your dog to find her toys** – If your dog likes toys, make up names for the toys and use the name consistently (e.g., yellow cat). Place "yellow cat" on the floor in front of your dog, then say its name out loud ("yellow cat"). Praise your dog as soon as she picks up yellow cat. If you do this with multiple toys, your dog can then learn to "find yellow cat" and bring it to you.

5. **Let your dog explore a bit on walks** – If your dog is allowed to sniff or explore while on walks, it will provide mental stimulation. You can still keep control of your dog by teaching "explore" as a command that means she has permission to sniff.

Photo Courtesy
of Sabrina Roybal

Keeping Your Dog Occupied While You Aren't Home

Bored dogs can be destructive dogs. But the reality is that as much as we might want to, we simply cannot be home with our Schnauzers all the time.

There are some things you can do to help your dog cope while you're gone. Note that some of these can be implemented if your dog is in a crate, but others only work if you choose not to crate your Schnauzer:

1. **Let your dog look out the window** – This is Puggles' "job" at our house, whether we are home or not. When we are home, we often leave the front door open so she can watch out the glass door. My bed is also pushed up against our bedroom window so she can "guard" outside from there. And guard she does. Any time a person gets too close to our house, or a FedEx truck even thinks of driving by, we know about it. Remember, Schnauzers are barkers, and they are serious about keeping their family safe from "evildoers." That said, Puggles did alert us to someone breaking into our car in the middle of the night, and thanks to her, the thieves were caught.

2. **Provide plenty of toys** – This includes the mental stimulation puzzles mentioned above, as well as whatever other toys your dog likes to play with. Just make sure your Schnauzer cannot tear the toy up because that can be dangerous if pieces are ingested.

3. **Leave the TV on** – This helps drown out the silence of an empty house. There are actually TV stations designed for dogs.

4. **Provide a playmate** – As we talked about in the last chapter, dogs are pack animals. Having a canine companion can help your dog deal with loneliness, although sometimes two simply get in bigger trouble than one. And your dog's companion doesn't necessarily have to be a dog. As I've said, Puggles and Boo are best friends.

5. **Install a doggy door** – Giving your Schnauzer the option of going in and outside on her own can help your dog stay physically and mentally stimulated when you are not home. It can also give your dog a means to escape should there be an emergency.

   However, doggy doors are not always the best option, depending on your situation. First, you need to have a fenced yard with no hazards, like a swimming pool. Second, recognize that while a doggy door will let your Schnauzer come in, it can also give unwanted critters easy access to your home. Finally, if your Schnauzer is able to come and go as he pleases, it can cause issues with your role as the alpha because you are giving up some control.

6. **Hire a dog sitter** – There are professional dog-sitting services with vetted professionals that are not incredibly expensive. You can also check with your vet or friends to see if they have recommendations. Having someone come and take your dog out during the day will help your Schnauzer get out some of that pent-up energy. It can also be helpful if you are not able to invest in the 60-plus minutes of recommended exercise yourself.

7. **Consider doggy daycare** – This option is a good one for some dogs, but not so much for others. Generally, puppies like to play with other dogs, and doggy daycare can be a great way for your pup to not only burn up energy during the day while you're gone but to also gain some important socialization time both with other dogs and new people. However, not all dogs enjoy being around other dogs, especially for extended periods of time. And of course, doggy daycare does cost money—although it may not be as much as you'd expect.

The Final Word

Schnauzers were bred to be active, both physically and mentally. Keeping your dog active will make her more confident and better behaved. No matter how you choose to do this, remember that Schnauzers were bred to be important members of the family. They will be happiest when being active involves participating with their "pack"—i.e., you and your family.

CHAPTER 10
Training Your Schnauzer

The time to start training your new Schnauzer ideally begins the moment you bring her home. That doesn't mean you have to start teaching commands as soon as she arrives, but you should definitely start setting boundaries. For example, it's confusing to your dog to let her sleep on the bed one night but not the next.

Your family needs to all be on board when it comes to setting boundaries and training. If, for example, you're teaching your dog not to beg at the dinner table, it's not fair to the Schnauzer for someone to slip her food when no one is looking.

Additionally, it's important to have clear and realistic expectations when it comes to training your new Schnauzer. First, training takes work both from you and your Schnauzer. If you take a training class, you have to practice the lessons between sessions. If you train your Schnauzer on your own, you have to take time regularly—preferably every day—to reinforce your training.

Second, you may be able to change your dog's behavior, but you cannot change her personality. Dogs, like people, have unique personalities that define who they are. For example, if your dog is grumpy around other dogs, you may be able to teach her not to growl, but you can't necessarily make her like being around other dogs.

Operant Conditioning Basics

Operant conditioning is a philosophy of dog training that originated with B.F. Skinner back in 1938. The general gist of Skinner's philosophy is that if you reward ("reinforce") an animal for a specific behavior, the animal is more likely to repeat that behavior.

Operant conditioning ideally focuses on rewards, but it can also include "punishments." These should never involve yelling, hitting, or anything that would scare your dog. But, for example, Puggles is learning that if she barks out of control while she's at the front door, we close her door so she can't see out. Or if she barks while looking out the bedroom window, I hold her muzzle and say "quiet" until she can sit without barking. (She's 11 years old, and I just started working on this a few months ago, but it's working! Puggles is proof you can still teach an old dog new tricks.)

In general, reinforcement—i.e., a positive—is used when you want to increase your Schnauzer's behavior. So when teaching tricks, rewards are used. Negative reinforcement is used when you want to decrease a behavior like barking.

Primary Reinforcements

"They are usually very eager to please their people and try very hard to figure out what you want. I'm not a fan of training with treats because they learn when you have something and when you don't and can learn to ignore you when you don't have treats. I prefer to reward with attention."

KELLY ROBISON
Belle Vista Schnauzers

In operant conditioning, there are two kinds of reinforcements: primary and secondary. Primary reinforcements, sometimes called "unconditional reinforcements," occur naturally and don't really require much by way of learning. For example, if you are teaching your dog to sit and she gets a treat every time she sits, sitting becomes a no-brainer. "Of course I'll sit if you give me that yummy treat!"

The most popular types of primary reinforcement are food, toys, and playtime. The type that works in your situation is going to largely depend on your Schnauzer's individual preferences. For example, my parents' dog loves to play with toys. It's his favorite thing to do. Puggles, on the other hand, could not care less about toys.

Primary reinforcements are typically how you will begin training. Give your dog a command, then reward when your Schnauzer obeys. However, the real trick in training is to teach your dog to obey without the need for primary reinforcement. This is where secondary reinforcements come into play.

The main types of secondary reinforcement are attention and praise. However, clickers are another good option when used correctly.

Clickers have a unique sound that dogs aren't used to hearing, so they pay more attention to the noise when they first hear it. The sound is also consistent, so it becomes easy for your dog to recognize. Clicker training works by clicking right when your dog does the behavior you're teaching, then immediately following up with a treat. There are plenty of YouTube videos that can give you more details on how to use a clicker for training.

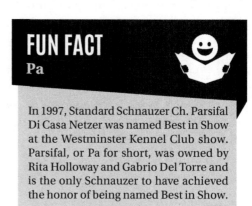

FUN FACT
Pa

In 1997, Standard Schnauzer Ch. Parsifal Di Casa Netzer was named Best in Show at the Westminster Kennel Club show. Parsifal, or Pa for short, was owned by Rita Holloway and Gabrio Del Torre and is the only Schnauzer to have achieved the honor of being named Best in Show.

Negative Reinforcement

Positive and negative reinforcement are more like math problems. With positive reinforcement, you add something. With negative reinforcement, you take something away. There's often a misunderstanding of what negative reinforcement is in dog training. Negative reinforcement is not the same as punishment. For example, a trainer might take away a reward if the dog does not follow through on a command.

Unfortunately, a lot of negative reinforcement involves pain. For example, a method that's commonly used in training retrievers involves an ear pinch or toe hitch that applies pain until the dog obeys a command. Another example is a pinch collar, where it hurts the dog to pull when walking, but the pain stops when the dog walks without pulling. A bark collar applies a shock when the dog barks, but the pain goes away as long as the dog stops barking.

The problem, beyond the obvious, is that any pain-based aversion technique can easily backfire. Studies have found that training involving pain can significantly increase a dog's stress, as well as potentially lead to increased aggression and future health issues. When training, look for ways to teach your dog without causing pain.

Timing is Everything

When training your Schnauzer, it's critical to use reinforcements at the time the act occurs. Dogs learn by association. They can understand that their immediate behavior creates an immediate consequence, good or bad.

Dogs do not understand punishment if it occurs after the fact. So if you find poop on the floor then rub your dog's nose in it, your dog will not make the connection. (Nor is it ever a good idea to do this, regardless of whether you catch your dog in the act or not!) Or calling your dog over after the fact to angrily show her the shoe she tore up will not make sense to your dog. In this case, you may accidentally teach your Schnauzer to associate "come" with something scary, and your dog will want to back away. Punishing your dog after the fact will not fix the negative behavior, but it may make her afraid of you.

"But my Schnauzer looked at me and hung her head in guilt." No, your Schnauzer was responding to your angry voice and body language, not to the fact that you scolded her because she specifically tore up the garbage.

*Photo Courtesy
of Kathryn Daniels*

Hiring a Trainer

Unfortunately, one of the biggest reasons dogs get brought to animal shelters is that the owners fell in love with a puppy, brought it home, but then never actually trained it. So a lot of dogs who are less than a year old are turned over to shelters. Although they are technically still puppies, by this point they are past the adorable baby stage; they are not housebroken; and they've picked up some bad habits. This, again, is why it's essential to start training your Schnauzer the moment you bring her home.

The good news is it really never is too late. However, there are some situations where a professional trainer should be brought in, especially if your dog is being aggressive towards your family, outsiders, or your other pets.

When it comes to training your dog, there are plenty of books and YouTube videos to give you guidance. The important thing is if you're going to do it yourself, you need to actually do it—and do it consistently.

Photo Courtesy
of Antti Suhonen

The best way to learn to safely control your dog, however, is to hire a dog trainer, whether that's in a private setting or in a group session. A trainer can help you teach your dog basic commands, how to walk on a leash, and can also help with difficult behaviors. I've been amazed by how quickly difficult dogs at the shelter behaved as soon as a professional came in to work with them.

Working with your Schnauzer every day, even if it's just for a few five-minute intervals, can make a huge difference. Training with your dog also builds bonding.

If you are simply wanting to teach your dog a few tricks, a group puppy class will likely be okay. The more serious your needs, however, the more you'll want to do your research for a qualified trainer. When choosing a trainer, ask for qualifications, references, and what type(s) of training methods the trainer uses. If you're needing help with a specific problem, ask how many sessions/weeks that type of problem typically takes to fix. (Most issues can be corrected fairly quickly.)

Your Behavior Matters!

"As long as a trainer is gentle, goes slow, praises often, and gives treats as rewards a Miniature Schnauzer will learn very fast. Each is different though, so some learn faster than others."

PAT A. HUNT
Alpats Miniature Schnauzers

"Dog" training is as much as about teaching you and your family as it is about teaching your dog how to behave. It's important to remember that dogs often act similar to their owners. Dogs are extremely in tune with their owners' emotions, and they often reflect their owners' behaviors. If the owner is anxious, for example, the dog will be too. If the owner is excited, so is the dog. If the owner yells or hits, the dog will be afraid.

When training, it's important to stay calm, even in stressful situations. (Practice deep-breathing techniques.) If you respond to your dog angrily, your dog will feel it. In these situations, dogs are typically more stressed and anxious than if you respond to your dog with sensitivity.

Your dog looks to you for guidance on how she should behave. She wants a strong but supportive and loving leader who sets boundaries. Remember, she is going to love you even if you tell her no.

CHAPTER 11
Basic Commands

In this chapter, we're going to get into some techniques for teaching your Schnauzer some basic commands. But first, let's take a quick glance back at why proper training is important, not just for you but also for your Schnauzer.

1. Training establishes you as the alpha.

2. It strengthens the bond between you and your Schnauzer.

3. It provides important mental and physical stimulation.

4. It helps keep your dog safe.

5. It builds your Schnauzer's confidence and trust.

6. It reduces stress both for you and your dog.

7. It makes your Schnauzer easier to control in new situations.

8. It allows you to better understand and read your dog's behavior.

9. It helps your Schnauzer behave better around guests or in public.

10. It helps protect your children and family members from being injured by your Schnauzer.

Photo Courtesy
of Jason Hamm

Picking the Right Reward

The most common reward option for dog training is a treat, and it's probably the easiest place to start. But it's not the only option, especially when it comes to more serious training. For example, K-9 dogs typically have to respond well to playing fetch in order to qualify for training. (Puggles could never be a K-9!) My parents' dog would be as happy with a toy as he would be with a treat. For some dogs, praise is enough.

For tougher training challenges, you're going to need to pull out better rewards. So, while little dog biscuits or "training treats" might be good enough for some basic commands, you might need a better treat or reward for certain others, especially when you are vying for your Schnauzer's attention.

Different Training Methods

Dog trainers have different training approaches and philosophies. These are the most popular options. Note that I never recommend using any kind of method that will cause your dog physical pain or discomfort.

1. **Classical Conditioning** – This is the old Pavlovian method that we learned about in school. Pavlov would ring a bell and then feed the dogs. Eventually, the dogs' mouths began to water every time they heard the bell.

Photo Courtesy of Deborah Holmes

While Pavlov's experiment was intentional, classical conditioning happens all the time, sometimes without us meaning for it to. For example, Puggles learned that any time I started changing clothes and putting on my tennis shoes, it meant we were going for a walk—even when it actually meant I was going to the gym. Another example—she now barks like crazy any time she sees an Amazon delivery truck drive by our house. That's because she is conditioned to think that Amazon trucks mean an outsider is coming to knock on our door.

Clicker Training is a type of classical conditioning, and works very well for most dogs. With clicker training, you use a small handheld device (i.e., the clicker) that you click every time your Schnauzer performs the desired task. The clicker always makes the exact same sound, which is why it's so effective. You click as soon as your dog correctly performs the task, then immediately give a treat. With time, your Schnauzer will learn to identify the clicker as the reward, making it easier to phase out treats.

2. **Operant Conditioning** – This method of dog training involves controlling the environment so that the dog's behavior has positive (receiving something) or negative (taking something away) consequences. For example, a dog that gets down at "down" receives a treat (positive reinforcement). A dog that does not get down is ignored or is gently pushed down until the dog stays down on its own.

How to Teach Basic Commands

Let's look at how to teach your Schnauzer some basic commands that every dog should learn.

Look at Me

This is a really important command as it's a way to lure your dog's attention away from distractions and to you. Here's how to teach it:

- Hold a treat in front of your Schnauzer's nose, then bring your hand with the treat slowly up to your nose so that it's between your eyes. Say, "Look at me."

- When your dog looks at your forehead, praise or click, then give your dog the treat.

- Repeat a few times, eventually switching so that you reward with your other hand.

- Now your dog should start to recognize both the words "look at me" and the hand signal (hand against your nose).

Sit

The "sit" command is one of the most important commands for your dog to learn as it helps your dog settle down in one spot to focus on you. It's also one of the easiest to teach. Here's how:

- Make sure you have treats ready. If you're using a clicker, have it in your hand.

- Select a training spot that is free from distractions.

- Hold up the treat just above your dog's nose.

- Say your dog's name, then "sit," and move the treat back towards your Schnauzer's ears. This usually causes the dog to sit.

- As soon as your dog sits, praise (or click) and immediately give your dog the treat.

Photo Courtesy
of Sunshine Herondale

- Repeat multiple times.
- Repeat without moving your hand backward over your dog's ears.

Lie Down

The method for teaching "lie down" is similar to teaching sit.

- Have your dog sit while you are holding a treat close to your dog's nose.
- Say "lie down" and bring the treat down slowly to the floor. Your dog will hopefully bring her elbows down, and she'll get into the correct position.
- Praise her (or click) when she does and immediately give her the treat.
- Repeat.

Come

This is a good one to teach after learning "sit" and "lie down." It's best to practice in an indoor area that's quiet, without distractions.

- Have your Schnauzer sit, and give her a treat like you normally would.
- While your dog is eating the first treat, back away a little bit.
- Say your Schnauzer's name and "come" while holding another treat.
- Praise/click when your dog comes, and give her a treat.
- Keep repeating this, stepping further away each time.

Stay

Stay is a really important command when it comes to both your dog's behavior and her safety. For example, if your Schnauzer gets out of the yard and starts to run into the street, knowing "stay" will hopefully help her stay safe while you get to her. However, "stay" is a harder command to learn.

With the "stay" command, your Schnauzer will stay sitting until you tell her to get up and do something else—like "come," which is why I suggested teaching come first. Note, however, it's actually better to teach your "release word" first—like "free" or "release"—which means it's now okay for your Schnauzer to move.

In this example, we're going to use "release." Again, you can also use "come," but it's a good idea to mix them up sometimes to make sure your Schnauzer truly understands that "stay" is a stand-alone command.

To teach "release:"

- Have your dog sit or lie down and then give her a treat.
- Say "stay," then immediately follow with "release" and reward when your dog moves.

- If your dog stays sitting, you might try stepping back or clapping your hands when you say "release" and follow with praise.

  Once you've done this a few times, you can move on to teaching "stay."
- Have your dog sit or lie down.
- Say "stay," then count to three, then "release."
- If your dog doesn't stay the full count, don't reward, but have your dog sit/lie down again and try it for a shorter duration.
- With time, you'll want to increase how long you require your dog to remain in the "stay" position.
- Next, you'll want to practice walking away from your dog (i.e., adding distance) while your dog remains in the "stay" position. This should be a slow transition, moving only a little bit farther away each time. If you are not having your dog "come," walk back to her before you release.
- Once you feel pretty confident about duration and distance, you can slowly add in some distractions. Start with something at home that's easy, then work on practicing in unfamiliar environments. You may need to use better treats when you're teaching your Schnauzer to stay during distractions.

Off/Down

- To teach this trick, you have to first catch your Schnauzer with her front paws or her entire body on something, like a counter or your legs.
- Say "off" or "down" while holding a treat in front of her nose.
- Lure your dog down with the treat.
- As soon as your dog is down or off, give the treat. (If you're using a clicker, click as you give the treat.)
- Repeat.

To make sure your dog really understands the trick, practice using the command when your dog is on different structures—sitting on the couch, paws on the table, etc.

Drop It

This is another important trick for your dog to learn in order to help keep her safe, as well as to help protect your belongings from getting chewed up. If your Schnauzer gets hold of something that could be dangerous, "drop it" will teach your dog to let go.

Before you start teaching this trick, you need to understand that it's a bad idea to pull a toy, treat, or other items from your dog's mouth. You also should never pull your dog's head or try to pry open her mouth to remove something. Your dog may bite you if you try this, or she may tighten her grip or even swallow the item as a result. If your dog won't let go of something dangerous, your best option is to give her treats so she'll choose to give up the item of her own free will.

When it comes to teaching "drop it," follow these steps:

- Offer your dog a favorite toy. Puggles is never much for toys, but she loves chews, so that's what I use. You may want to let your Schnauzer play with the toy for a few seconds before you start training if your dog is super excited, but don't wait so long that she gets bored.

- While your Schnauzer is holding the toy in her mouth, hold up a treat next to her nose and say, "Drop it."

- As soon as she releases the toy, give her a treat (and click if using a clicker).

- Repeat several times.

To make sure your dog understands the command, practice it while your dog is chewing on different items and in different settings.

Heel

This is a classic trick to teach your dog, and will make walking your Schnauzer much more enjoyable. While it's not required, you may want to teach your dog to stay on your left side, as this is how it's done in dog competitions. Here's how to teach heel:

- Start by walking around your house.
- Call your Schnauzer by name, then point to the side that you want her to walk next to you on and say "heel."

- Hold your hand with the treats next to your chest so she won't be lured by the food while you walk.

- The moment your Schnauzer comes next to you on the correct side, praise with a "yes" (or click) and give a treat using the hand next to your dog. This will keep her from crossing in front of you to get to the treat.

- Repeat, slowly adding some new challenges like walking faster, turning around, etc., so your Schnauzer will have to find the position again.

- If your dog gets distracted, use the "look at me" cue to get her to refocus.

Advanced Commands

This chapter only goes into what is considered basic obedience training. Don't rush through the basics. It's better to take your time and make sure your Schnauzer has a solid, consistent grasp on each element of basic obedience training before moving forward.

Once your Schnauzer performs these commands consistently and in a variety of settings, you may want to press forward into more advanced training. Schnauzers—like all dogs—enjoy having a job, and it helps them bond with their families. Dogs can learn a variety of tricks, including elements of agility training, service training, and more. It's a great way for you and your Schnauzer to continue spending time together.

FUN FACT
Versatile Companion Dogs

Versatile Companion Dog (VCD) Titles were developed by the American Kennel Club to recognize dog and handler teams who are talented in obedience, tracking, and agility events. The VCD title was created in 2001, but the first time a Versatile Companion Champion Title (VCCH) was awarded was in 2009. In 2017, a Standard Schnauzer and Giant Schnauzer each earned VCD titles.

CHAPTER 12
Dealing With Unwanted Behaviors

Throughout this book we've talked about the fact that you have to set the rules for your Schnauzer right from the beginning. As an animal shelter volunteer, it breaks my heart—and frankly, ticks me off—to see so many older puppies brought back to the shelter because the owners "didn't have time to train."

Your Schnauzer will not learn your rules without your leadership. Breaking your dog's bad behaviors is your responsibility.

What is "Bad Behavior" in Dogs?

In dogs, "bad" behavior typically refers to when a dog excessively practices annoying conduct despite your attempts to correct the dog's behavior. Some of the most common negative behaviors include the following:

- Barking
- Begging
- Biting
- Chewing
- Digging
- Jumping up
- Pulling
- Whining.

For the sake of this chapter, I'm not referring just to occasionally doing these things. I'm referring to when these things are incessant and difficult to correct.

Finding the Root of the Problem

Years ago, I had two beagles that lived with me in my apartment. I would take them out in the morning, then again when I got home from work, and before bed. They were both potty trained and had no problems for the first two years that I had them.

Then one day, I realized one of the dogs had urinated on my bed. Gross, right? It started becoming a common thing, so I started coming home for lunch to let the dogs out, thinking that maybe one of them couldn't hold it. (Why he chose my bed, I don't know.) Then one day he jumped on my bed and urinated on it right in front of me! I took the dog to the vet, but there was no physical reason for it, such as a UTI. It could have been due to separation anxiety, or he may have been marking his territory—on MY bed!

Another problem I've seen through my shelter experience is dogs who are extra submissive will often roll over on their back, then accidentally urinate on themselves. This is especially common with dogs who've been abused. And sometimes dogs are just so happy to see you that they wet themselves.

Photo Courtesy of Priscilla Boles

Let's look at another example. There was a lab mix at the animal shelter who would growl at anyone who came near his cage. The staff had to put a warning sign on his cage so no one would go in. However, after a little while, I found out he was fine if you just opened the door and went in. He was wonderful if he was out of the kennel. He was just scared and felt threatened when people stood in front of the kennel door. He wasn't aggressive or mean. He was scared.

One more story—although this one is with a cat. The cats at the shelter are in open rooms with other cats/kittens of the same sex and size. One day, there was a horrible orange tabby kitten in the room. It would not only hiss and scratch any kitten that got near it, but it would growl and attack all the other kittens. It was the meanest kitten I'd ever seen—or so I thought. Then they took it to the vet, and it turned out its belly was swollen from an infection. The kitten was in pain! After a few days at the vet, that kitten came back playful and purring. He wasn't mean. He was sick.

My point is that negative behavior isn't always because an animal is being "bad." When dogs are anxious, stressed, hurt, or sick, they may act out. So if your Schnauzer suddenly starts acting differently, you may want to call the vet.

Bad Behavior Prevention

If you know that something specific triggers your Schnauzer's bad behavior, you may first just want to remove that trigger when possible. For example, if you want your dog to stop begging for food, don't give her table scraps.

You can also try to decondition your dog to certain triggers. For example, if your Schnauzer automatically barks like crazy at the sound of a doorbell, there are apps that play doorbells randomly to condition your dog to the sound so she gets used to the noise.

Some behaviors—like digging—may be because your Schnauzer needs to burn off some pent-up energy. Taking your dog for more walks, teaching her tricks, or going to the dog park can burn off some of that excess energy and help reduce problems.

Finally, if your dog is doing certain things for attention, like jumping up—or in my case, Puggles will come over and repeatedly touch my leg with her paw—ignoring can be a good way to get her to stop. Note that yelling at your Schnauzer is not a good solution because even though it's negative attention, it's still attention. It can also make your dog anxious and frightened of you. Finally, if you yell at your Schnauzer for barking, she may very well think you are joining in the fun and barking too.

How to Keep Your Dog from Barking

"I've found that some can get a little too Barky. It's their nature to alarm. Just keep working with them using a reward system that rewards being quiet at specific times. I combine this with crate training. My Schnauzers know that when they are in their crate they need to be silent."

LINDA RODES
Sedor Kennel

Schnauzers are big-time barkers. In my case, it's my Schnauzer's worst quality. (She also "squeals" really loudly when she's excited, and it's ear piercing!)

I'll be honest and say this is a problem I have not solved in the 11 years we've had Puggles, although I've worked on it more this year, and it's helping—if I catch her about to bark.

The method I read to use was to hold her muzzle when she started barking and say "Quiet," then give her a treat when she quits barking. With time, I've been able to just touch her and say "quiet" without holding her muzzle. Sometimes I can just say "quiet," and she'll stay quiet.

There are other methods that are recommended. These include:

- **Reward for "quiet," and ignore when she barks** – When your dog barks, wait until she is quiet. Don't look at her or say anything. But as soon as she stops barking, say "quiet" and "good dog," then reward. (If you use a clicker, click as soon as she stops barking.)
- **Teach your dog "speak" first** – To do this, do something that you know will make your Schnauzer bark, like knocking on the door or ringing the

doorbell. As soon as you see your dog bark, say "speak" and use a hand signal of some sort (whatever signal you choose to use), then give a treat. Repeat this multiple times, then try without the knock. When your dog can speak on command, it's time to teach quiet by adding the word "quiet" and rewarding when your dog stops barking.

- **Remove the temptation** – We leave our front door open a large percentage of the day so that Puggles can see out the glass door. If she starts barking at anyone outside and doesn't stop on "quiet," we shut the door. If your dog starts barking at something in the yard, bring your Schnauzer inside.

Photo Courtesy
of Sunshine Herondale

One thing you should not do is use a bark collar. These are designed to teach dogs not to bark by reacting to the vibration of your dog's vocal cords and giving a negative response, such as a high-pitched sound or shocking your dog. These responses add to a dog's anxiety rather than fix the behavior, and can cause your dog discomfort or even pain.

How to Properly Correct Your Dog

Unwanted behaviors can be corrected. If you have identified that a behavior is not due to a medical issue—including anxiety—there are some things you can do to fix the problem. Bear in mind that you have to catch your Schnauzer in the act. Punishing your dog for going potty in the house or chewing up your favorite pair of shoes will do no good if you try it after the fact.

- **Never yell or hit** – Yelling and hitting will only scare your dog. As I mentioned before, if your dog is wanting your attention, yelling may encourage your dog to continue the behavior because negative attention is still better than no attention. Instead, you need to stay calm, keep your voice level and low, and move slowly and deliberately. Otherwise your Schnauzer may think you are trying to play.

- **Redirect** – Dogs, and especially puppies, will chew. Likewise, digging and chasing animals is instinctive, and as such, you may not be able to completely eliminate the behavior. In these cases, redirecting your dog to a more suitable object—like a chew toy or a specific area of your yard where digging is allowed—is a better option.

- **Teach "No!" or "Stop!"** – Pick a word to serve as an interruption command and use that to get your dog's attention. You should not yell, but you can use a loud, firm voice for the command word.

- **Practice** – Not only will practicing with your dog help teach your dog what is and is not appropriate behavior, but it will help you bond with your Schnauzer and reinforce your role as the alpha. Also, some bad behaviors result just from an unfamiliar environment. The more your dog gets acclimated to the sights, smells, and sounds of a situation, the better behaved she may be with time.

- **Be consistent** – For training to work, everyone has to be on board. For example, you can't expect to teach your dog not to beg at the dinner table if one family member is sneaking her food when no one is looking.

When Should I Hire a Dog Trainer?

A lot of dog behaviors can be fixed by using the strategies above, but there are times when a dog's problem behavior is more than you can handle. If the dog's behavior is a danger to you, others, or the dog, then hiring a trainer may be the best option.

At the animal shelter, the staff is somewhat trained in how to handle problem behaviors, but there are some instances when a volunteer professional trainer will be called in. For example, we've had some large, hyper dogs that would jump up or nip (for play) to the point that they were not safe to be around. One dog, Scooby, would literally bounce off the walls of his kennel. They were all sweet dogs but not well behaved, and too hard for volunteers or potential adopters to handle.

Another large dog was as sweet as could be with people but

Photo Courtesy of Kaycie Vidrine PhotographybyKV

hated other dogs. She would bark and growl aggressively at every dog—including puppies—when we tried to take her out, which made handling very difficult. Finally, there were some dogs that would growl or snap at humans. In most cases, a little bit of training fixed those issues as well. These dogs were too much for us to handle on our own, but when a dog trainer came in, they were completely different dogs within minutes. It was incredible!

If your dog growls or is aggressive—even if it's just food aggressive—you may want to bring in a trainer. It's not worth the risk of you or someone else getting hurt.

If your Schnauzer bolts out the door every time it's open, that's putting your dog at risk, and a trainer might be needed.

Or, if there's just a negative behavior that you cannot fix on your own, it's best to call in an expert.

CHAPTER 13
Traveling with Schnauzers

"Miniature Schnauzers love to travel, it can be a true joy for them. Bring along potty bags for when you make a rest stop. Make sure you have crate or appropriate seating for their safety."

RHONDA SMITH
Heavenly Miniature Schnauzer

To your Schnauzer, you and your family are everything, and your dog is going to want to be with you everywhere you go, whether it be a quick trip in the car or a cross-country journey. With some preparation and training, traveling with your dog can be a great experience for both you and your Schnauzer.

Dog Carriers and Car Restraints

While your Schnauzer may love to sit in the front seat and stick her head out the window, that's really not the safest option for you or your dog. In fact, in some states, it's now illegal and considered a violation of animal cruelty laws.

If you were to get into an accident, your unrestrained Schnauzer could easily get injured—or worse. If allowed to run loose in the car, your Schnauzer can be a distraction for whoever is driving, adding more risk for an accident, as well as a "distracted driving" charge. Additionally, if you were to get into an accident, your dog might panic and dart

STORY
Lights, Camera, Schnauzer!

Arno, a Standard Schnauzer, was the constant companion of actor Errol Flynn during the 1930s. Both on stage and off, Arno accompanied Flynn almost everywhere and is said to have gotten almost as much media coverage as Flynn's romantic partners at the time. One of Arno's pastimes was riding on Flynn's yacht, Sirocco, and snapping at the flying fish. In 1941, Arno is believed to have fallen off the yacht and been washed away. He was given a naval burial at sea by the Coast Guard.

out of the car, especially if there's a broken window. That leads to the added risk of your Schnauzer getting lost or hit by a vehicle. Finally, a scared dog can make it harder for emergency responders to get to you or your family members if you are injured and incapacitated.

Besides accidents, there are other dangers of driving with an unrestrained dog. Your Schnauzer might jump out of an open window, get injured by debris while hanging her head outside, or if you are in an accident, a deployed airbag can cause serious injuries.

One of the best things you can do to keep you, your family, and your Schnauzer safe while in the car is to keep the dog restrained. There are two primary ways to do this: dog carriers and car restraints.

Dog carriers are typically the safest option for your dog, but you need to select one that is specially designed for vehicle travel as these have been safety certified to withstand crash tests. Crates made from aluminum, with fiberglass reinforcements or other similarly durable materials, are safest.

Your vehicle crate should be the right size for your dog. You want your dog to be comfortable, but the crate shouldn't be too big. A good rule of thumb is to measure your dog's sitting height (from head to toe) and standing length, then add two inches both ways. Additionally, you want to make sure the crate will fit snugly in your vehicle. The less the crate can move, the safer for your dog. Finally, select a crate that allows air circulation so that your dog can breathe, as well as one that offers good insulation so your dog is comfortable no matter the temperature. Some crates even offer crash bags to provide protection if the crate breaks.

Another option for helping to keep your dog safe while in the car is a dog restraint system. These dog harnesses are specially designed to be used with your vehicle's seat-belt strap. The harness should be stronger than the one you would typically use for walking. Once the harness is strapped on correctly, the seat belt slides through a piece on the harness across your dog's back. Look for a car harness that has been certified by CPS standards, which uses the same standards to test child car seats.

Preparing Your Schnauzer for Car Rides

Getting your dog used to successfully riding in the car requires training and repetition, setting rules from the start. The sooner you get your dog used to riding in the car, the better.

Start by letting your Schnauzer explore your vehicle while it is parked. Note, it's a good idea to bring a blanket or toy that she only can have in the

Photo Courtesy of Claudia Dancila

car. Next, put your dog in her crate or strap her in with the harness, then turn on the engine and the radio (softly) so she can experience what the car feels like when it's turned on. Next, move backward and forward a little in the driveway, so your dog gets used to movement. Finally, it's time to go for a real ride.

The more you can take your dog with you, the better. If your Schnauzer only gets to ride in the car for trips to the vet or to the groomer, the more she will naturally learn to associate the car with negative experiences. Driving her to the dog park or to another fun walking location can help her look forward to the car and reduce her anxiety.

Tips and Tricks for Traveling

If you are taking your dog on a long trip, bear the following two key things in mind:

- Make sure your Schnauzer is wearing a collar with her name and your contact number, in case she somehow escapes. Also, it's a great idea to get your dog microchipped. I know from my shelter experience that a microchip makes finding dog's owners much easier!

- If you're going on a long trip, make sure you keep your vet's records and information with you in case there's an emergency and another vet needs to see your dog's info.

Things to take with you on a road trip with your dog:

- Food and water from home. Your Schnauzer is probably going to be stressed from being on the road and in a new environment, which can cause tummy issues. Feeding your Schnauzer the same food and treats she gets at home can help. Also, anyone who's traveled knows that water can taste different in other areas of the country, and new water could also upset your dog's stomach. Try to pack at least enough water that you can ease your Schnauzer into the new water by mixing it with your home's water at first.

- Collapsible bowls
- Leash and/or harness
- Any medications
- Blanket or towel
- Brush and shampoo
- Poop bags
- Treats
- Crate (if you're staying some-where overnight).

Try to feed your dog a few hours before getting into the car or wait until you arrive. Don't offer food while you're on the road if you can avoid it, in case your Schnauzer gets car sick. Before you start out, take her on a long walk to wear her down so she can rest in the car.

Be sure to give water frequently, and also stop regularly for potty breaks.

Make sure you keep your dog cool enough so that she doesn't overheat. You may want to purchase a window shade if she's going to be in the sun.

Finally, never leave your dog in the car alone, especially in extreme hot or cold temperatures. In some states, it's actually illegal.

Once you reach your destination, try to do things similarly to the way you would at home. Take your dog on a long walk if possible.

Photo Courtesy
of Jason Hamm

Flying with Your Schnauzer

If you're going on vacation and want to take your Schnauzer along, you're not alone. Over one million pet owners in the US take their pets on flights with them each year. Depending on the size of your Schnauzer, she may be able to fly in the cabin with you. To be considered a "carry-on item," your dog must fit in a carry-on case that fits the airline's size rules, and that case must be able to fit under the seat in front of you. Plan to pay extra for bringing your pooch.

If your Schnauzer qualifies as a certified service animal, airlines must allow you to fly your dog with you at no extra charge. They may require documentation to verify that your disability requires service animal support. Note that airlines often do not count emotional support animals as service dogs.

Each airline has its own policies, so you'll need to check with their website or call the airline directly before flying. For example, some airlines may not allow dogs on longer flights, dogs under a certain age, and certain breeds. (Schnauzers likely are not a banned breed.)

If your Schnauzer is too big for the cabin, she will have to ride with the baggage. The cost is often based on the weight and size of the dog. It can be expensive. Also, some airlines will not allow pets to travel as cargo if the temperature is too hot or too cold.

Whether your Schnauzer is riding with you as carry-on or with the baggage, you'll need a carrier. Soft-sided carriers are better for carry-on since they are flexible and easier to fit under the seat. Hard-sided carriers with ventilation holes are required for the cargo section. Airlines require that the carrier be big enough for your dog to comfortably stand up, turn around, and lie down. Let your dog spend some time getting used to the carrier well before your trip. Also, make sure you label your carrier with your dog's name and include your contact information. You may want to write the info on the carrier itself, as well as tag the carrier.

Before heading to the airport, take your Schnauzer to the vet for a checkup. She needs to be up to date on all vaccines and flea treatments and should ideally be checked over for any other potential health concerns. You may also want to have your dog groomed before your trip so she'll be more comfortable.

While it may be tempting to give your dog a sedative of some sort when flying, most veterinarians don't recommend this. Sedatives will affect your Schnauzer's brain so that she'll be more confused, which can make her more stressed out. They also reduce your dog's heart rate, breathing, and body temperature, which can be dangerous, especially at high altitudes. Talk to your veterinarian about other possible options.

On the day of your flight, most airlines recommend getting there two hours early with your pet. Make sure you have all your dog's paperwork where you can easily reach it. US airports that have more than 10,000 passengers per year are required by law to provide a "pet relief" area. There is usually one per terminal. Take your Schnauzer there before and after your flight.

Dog-Friendly Hotels

When it comes to keeping your dog in a hotel, it's smart to do your homework. The internet has plenty of websites that list dog-friendly hotels, and travel sites can give you insights into other travelers' experiences.

You should never try to sneak your dog into a hotel. It is stressful, unethical, and can get you in trouble. There are plenty of dog-friendly options these days, including some large hotel chains. So do your research, and do it right. Also, be honest about how big your dog is. Some hotels only allow dogs up to a certain size. It's better to find one where your dog will be welcome.

When you make your reservation, ask for a ground-floor room. This makes it easier to take your dog to go potty.

Dog-friendly hotels may require a deposit and will likely charge extra for letting your little pooch come along. Some let dogs stay free. Some charge a whopping fee. Make sure you find out the cost beforehand.

When you arrive, go for a long walk before going inside. This will help wear your dog down a bit, as well as help her adapt to the new surroundings as she gets to sniff around. When you get to your room, have your Schnauzer sit before you open the door, then walk in first. This will help her know that it's a safe place. Once she enters, walk around the room

Photo Courtesy of Merry Morrissy-Karp

with her while she explores. Again, this will help her adapt and feel secure.

After you are in the room and she's explored, give her something she knows—like a toy or a blanket. You ideally want to bring your dog's bed and/or blanket and crate with you. Your dog will feel more at ease with her own belongings. If you are going to let your dog sleep on the bed with you, it's nice to bring a sheet with you to cover the bedspread. While you don't have to worry about your Schnauzer shedding, she still may get the bedspread dirty.

Hopefully, your Schnauzer is potty trained. If not, bring potty pads and take her out frequently to do her business.

It's best not to use the hotel tub to wash your dog. While, with your Schnauzer, you won't be leaving fur in the tub, you will be leaving dirt, and potentially wet-dog smell all over the room. If you do use the tub, bring something to clean it up with when you're finished.

As a Schnauzer owner, I know all too well that barking can be a problem. Hopefully you will have worked on barking before you arrive at the hotel. Even so, do not leave your dog alone in the room without you because she will be more likely to bark and cry while you're gone. She may also tear up the furniture, your suitcase, and whatever else she can find.

Some hotels will not allow you to leave your dog alone in the room, and they also will not clean your room if your dog is inside. It's really best to take her with you. If you have to leave her, try to do it only for a short time. Remember that your Schnauzer is in a new, scary place without her family. Turn the TV on to help provide some white noise, and then put her in her crate.

Pet Sitters vs. Boarding

If you are going to be going out of town and are leaving your Schnauzer at home, you have to figure out who is going to take care of her. Assuming you don't have family or neighbors to come to feed her and let her out, you will need to either hire a pet sitter or board her.

Pet sitters may come to stay at your house, but you might also just hire them to come by a few times a day—especially first thing in the morning and later in the evening—to let your Schnauzer go out and use the bathroom, make sure she's fed, and possibly take her on a walk. There are some advantages to pet sitters, the most obvious being that your dog will still be in the comfort of her home, and she will get one-on-one attention from the sitter. If the sitter doesn't stay at your house, your Schnauzer may be lonely, but at least she's not lonely and in a new environment. With a pet sitter, you can also provide specific instructions on how to care for your dog. You may even ask the sitter to take photos of your dog when she visits to make sure she's actually going there when she's supposed to!

The downside is pet sitters are expensive, especially if they are staying with your dog. If your pet sitter only comes to check in on your Schnauzer, it may cost you less, but if there's an emergency with your dog, the sitter won't necessarily be there when it happens.

Boarders are professional facilities where you can take your Schnauzer to stay while you are gone. Some boarders have different-sized areas—from crate-sized to larger kennels with indoor and outdoor runs—where your dog will stay. Others (house boarders) may keep several dogs in their home overnight, almost like a doggy daycare sleepover. You will want to make sure your dog is well socialized with other dogs before going this route. Home boarding is more expensive than a regular boarding facility but probably less expensive than having someone stay at your house.

No matter where you board your Schnauzer, the place will likely have several dogs boarding there at the same time as your dog, so it will be loud—which can be scary. Your dog will need to be up-to-date on her shots, especially for kennel cough. Some boarders provide a certain amount of playtime in the cost, while with others it is optional and costs extra. You will not be able to make a lot of requirements with how they take care of your dog.

Whether you choose to use a pet sitter or a boarder, make sure you find one that is reputable. Pet sitters should have references, and you may want to run a background check yourself or use a pet-sitting service that provides background checks. You will want to meet the person prior to heading out of town, and make sure you feel comfortable leaving your Schnauzer in her hands.

If you're taking your dog to a boarder, read reviews and ask for references. Tour the facility ahead of time before you agree to take your Schnauzer there.

Whether you decide to take your Schnauzer with you on vacation or leave her at home (or board her), do it right. Take the time and effort to train her, and spend the money to keep her safe.

CHAPTER 14
Nutrition

Importance of Good Diet

"Schnauzers are prone to pancreatitis so never feed them any pork products. Table scraps should not be fed except in small quantities! A high quality dog food and prepared doggie snacks should be all they are ever fed! Diet is so important to keeping a Schnauzer healthy."

BARBARA DURRANCE
Show Stopper Schnauzers

S tarting your Schnauzer's diet off on the right foot is essential to keeping your new pup in tip-top shape. The earlier you cave in and start giving your dog table scraps, the harder the habit is to break. While, yes, people food will make your dog super happy for the moment, most human food is actually hurting your Schnauzer's health.

Schnauzers are prone to certain health issues, with pancreatitis being right there at the top. We'll talk more about pancreatitis in Chapter 17, but in brief: it typically results from too much fat in a dog's diet, and a lot of those table scraps are high in fat. "Fresh vegetables make a nice treat, but otherwise, table scraps should be off-limits," warns Kelly Robison of Belle Vista Schnauzers.

The Right Foods for Your Schnauzer

The amount of food you feed your dog is going to depend on how much your Schnauzer weighs. Here is a general guide based on her weight:

- Miniature Schnauzers (up to 20 pounds): 1 to 1 1/3 cups
- Standard Schnauzers (30 to 45 pounds): 1 1/2 to 2 2/3 cups
- Giant Schnauzers (50-75 pounds): 2 2/3 to 3 1/3 cups.

Just like with humans, the more active your Schnauzer is, the more she can eat.

In addition to weight, your dog's age is going to impact the nutrient she needs.

Because puppies have more energy, they need higher protein and fat content, typically about twice as much as adults. Some puppy food will also contain DHA (docosahexaenoic acid), a fatty acid additive that is important for your puppy's heart, brain, and eye development. DHA can be found naturally in oily fish like salmon, or there are supplements you can provide as treats or add to food. Fatty acids are also believed to help with skin conditions, and Schnauzers are prone to skin allergies, so fatty acids can be a good additive no matter your dog's age.

After the first year, your Schnauzer's nutritional needs will change. At this point, you'll want her diet to have at least 10 percent protein. She can have up to 50 percent carbohydrates, which should include a fiber content of 2 to 5 percent.

As your Schnauzer grows older, she will likely become less active, and her metabolism will slow down. This means she will need around 20 percent fewer calories than when she was a younger adult dog. Senior foods not only accommodate for the caloric change, but they can provide more nutrition to promote joint health. Examples include glucosamine and chondroitin sulfate, which are believed to help with cartilage and joint health. Giant Schnauzers, like other large breeds, are also more prone to joint issues, so these are good additives for their foods. L-carnitine is another additive sometimes included in senior dog food to help with cognitive function.

When it comes to diet, you want to make sure whatever you feed your dog is well balanced in nutrition and contains protein, fiber, and carbohydrates. Here's a recommended breakdown in nutrition:

Protein – Adult dogs need to get at least 10 percent of their daily calories from protein, such as poultry, fish, and eggs. Watch out for fattier meats like beef and some pork.

Carbohydrates – As low or no-carb diets have become popular among humans, "grain-free" dog foods have begun hitting the market. However, the Food and Drug Administration has warned that grain-free dog foods can potentially have serious side effects in some dogs. This includes a rare but life-threatening problem called dilated cardiomyopathy. Grain-free foods

can also cause liver and kidney problems. Therefore, most vets do not recommend a grain-free diet. Carbohydrates are also important for adding fiber to a dog's diet. Carbs can come from plants, grains (i.e., rice, oats, barley), and legumes. Wheat products can lead to weight gain, as well as skin problems, so watch out for them.

Fats – While you don't want to overdo it with fats for your Schnauzer, they are an important part of your dog's diet. This is because fats provide energy, help with vitamin absorption, and support cell function. They also help prevent dry, itchy skin, which is a common problem with Schnauzers. However, again, you need to be careful with providing too many or the wrong kinds of fats, so avoid table scraps and keep your Schnauzer from becoming obese. It only takes one high-fat meal to trigger pancreatitis, which is what we've recently had happen to my Schnauzer who is older but not overweight. Too much fat also can make your dog obese, and Schnauzers are prone to diabetes. Therefore, fats should make up just 5 percent of your dog's diet, and should include omega-3 fatty acids.

Calcium and Vitamin D – Just like with humans, these nutrients help make strong teeth and bones, so you'll want to include small amounts in your Schnauzer's diet. However, too much calcium can lead to bladder stones, particularly in male Schnauzers.

What Type of Food is Best for My Schnauzer?

When purchasing commercial dog food, look for labels that say things like "chicken and rice" as opposed to "chicken dinner." Chicken and rice means that 95 percent of the ingredients are from chicken and rice, while words like "dinner" mean the amount of actual chicken can be as little as 25 percent.

Also, look for the Association of American Feed Control Officials (AAFCO) statement, indicating that the food is "complete and balanced." The AAFCO follows the Nutritional Research Council (NRC) to ensure that dog food reaches at least the minimum levels of protein, carbohydrates, fiber, fat, minerals, and vitamins required to meet the energy needs of specific dogs at various life stages.

When looking for the amount of nutrients in a dog food, manufacturers are only required to list the minimum amounts of protein, fat, fiber, and moisture in the ingredient list. The amounts may vary by batch.

Finally, always look at the ingredient list, paying special attention to the first five or six listed. These are placed in order of weight, so if it lists "corn" as the first ingredient and "chicken" fifth, you know there's more corn than chicken. Note that "meal" usually refers to organ meat, such as hearts, livers, and kidneys, where the water and fat have been removed.

Types of Commercial Dog Food

"Miniature Schnauzers need a diet that is low in fat. Try to find a high end dog food that has under 18% crud fat. There are some very good foods out there for them, you just need to feed them a good quality food as it can and will give them a better life. We always steam extra veggies as schnauzer love their vegetables."

RHONDA SMITH
Heavenly Miniature Schnauzer

I recently learned that with cats, most veterinarians recommend wet food because it gives them more water. However, wet food is not necessarily better—or worse—for dogs. So a lot of it is a matter of preference and your dog's specific needs. Let's look at the advantages and disadvantages of both:

Dry Food

Dry food, typically, is just less work to feed your Schnauzer. It's less messy. It's easier to store. It's simpler to measure. It doesn't go bad if your dog doesn't eat it all. And it's typically less expensive. Dry food can also help your dog's teeth stay cleaner.

Another advantage is that many dry foods have a low-fat content. While this may not be great for some high-energy breeds, you really need to watch the amount of fat you give your Schnauzer, especially as she gets older. Most dry foods are higher in carbohydrate content, so if you want something with increased protein or fat, it typically costs more. Also, you need to watch out for cheap dog foods that contain red dye.

As for the disadvantages, the biggest issues with dry food are that dogs often don't like the taste as much, and older dogs with bad teeth may have a hard time eating it. (I will sometimes add water to ours, but it does have to get eaten or thrown out after a few hours, or it will begin to rot.)

Wet Dog Food

Dogs often love wet food because it tastes better. Wet food is much higher in moisture, which is important if your Schnauzer doesn't drink enough or if she has urinary tract issues. It also helps your dog feel fuller faster. If your dog needs to lose weight, wet food is a good way to help her feel like she's getting more food than she really is. Active and younger dogs may also benefit from the higher protein content in wet food to help them build muscle.

On the downside, wet foods typically need to be refrigerated after opening and are only good for a day or two, so there may be waste. Wet food can lead to plaque buildup on your dog's teeth since there is not the roughness of dry food to help clean teeth. Wet food usually has higher fat content, which, again, is not a good thing for Schnauzers.

From a practical standpoint, wet food will make your Schnauzer's beard really dirty. Finally, if you start your dog on wet food, it may be hard to transition to dry later on because it does taste better.

Photo Courtesy
of Colleen Bedford

Fresh Foods

This is a relatively new trend, and one I've started trying with my dog since she has recently developed what the vet believes is pancreatitis.

Fresh foods are usually found in a small refrigerated section in the pet aisle or pet store. There are also options that will deliver fresh meals directly to your door. All of these types of dog foods are made from human-grade foods, which theoretically means they are healthier. They are not as messy

Photo Courtesy
of Sarah LaGrone

as wet food, which is good from a Schnauzer beard standpoint, and the real ingredients are listed.

These foods state that they come "straight from the farm," using 100 percent farm-raised meat (chicken, beef, or fish), plus all-natural vegetables and fruits. They are preservative-free and contain no meat powders or other fillers. As you might expect, they are more expensive than most dry or wet foods.

Homemade Food

Another growing trend is to make your dog's food from scratch. The advantage is that you know what your dog is consuming, and it is therefore considered a healthier option than commercially made products.

Meats –A general rule of thumb is to use lean, ideally organic, grass-fed meat or fish as the base for your dog's homemade meal. Some people will use raw meat. However, these are more susceptible to bacteria. When choosing your proteins, you really want to try to keep the fat content to 5 percent.

When Puggles had a pancreatitis flare-up recently, we were told to only feed her boiled skinless chicken breasts with the fat removed. Skinless white meat chicken is a good option, as is turkey, including ground. If the meat needs added oil, use only a little bit of coconut or olive oil. Once you've finished cooking the meat, crumble it or dice it into small pieces.

Next, you can add vegetables, such as carrots, peas, squash (yellow or butternut), green beans, cucumbers, and sweet potatoes. Pumpkin, including canned (but not pie filling), is a great filler and good for digestion. Boiled spinach can be used but should be limited. The same goes for broccoli. White potatoes are okay in small amounts, but you should remove the peel and any green areas beneath the peel. You can also add fruits like apples, bananas, unsweetened applesauce, pears, and blueberries. For the fruits and veggies, boil or steam them together, then mash with a potato masher.

For carbs, whole grains are best. Rice, oats, sweet potatoes, and white potatoes are good options. As stated earlier, some dogs have wheat allergies. With the potatoes, you need to remove the skins. Oats and rice are good for adding texture and helping hold the food together.

When putting the food together, here's a general rule: For every cup of meat, add three-fourths of a cup of vegetables (with or without a few fruits) and half a cup of carbs. If you need more moisture, adding warmed-up pumpkin helps it all stick together, and it counts as a vegetable.

You can mix together large batches, then freeze them in small containers so you aren't having to cook every day. Just move the next day's serving into the refrigerator overnight so it can defrost.

Human Foods that are Bad for Dogs

"Schnauzers can be prone to pancreatitis and kidney/bladder issues which can be exacerbated by too much fat or protein in the diet."

KELLY ROBISON
Belle Vista Schnauzers

Here is a list of human foods to avoid giving your dog, according to the American Humane Society:

- Alcoholic beverages
- Apple seeds
- Apricot pits
- Artificial sweeteners, which can be toxic to dogs
- Avocados
- Cherry pits
- Candy
- Chocolate. It's toxic!
- Coffee
- Garlic
- Grapes
- Gum
- Hops (used in home beer brewing)
- Macadamia nuts
- Moldy foods
- Mushroom plants
- Mustard seeds
- Onions and onion powder
- Peach pits
- Potato leaves and stems (green parts). It's best to remove the skins.
- Raisins
- Rhubarb leaves
- Salt
- Tea
- Tomato leaves and stems
- Walnuts
- Xylitol
- Yeast dough.

Human snacks that are okay to give your dog include anything mentioned in the homemade food section of this book. Peanut butter without added sugar and absolutely without any xylitol (this is toxic to dogs and is in a lot of peanut butter, so read the labels!) is okay in moderation, as are small amounts of cheese. These foods can be good ways to hide medication if needed.

For Schnauzers, low-fat dog treats are best. Rawhides and other chews may be okay in moderation. Do not give your dog pig ears or other dried pork treats because they are high in fat.

Managing Your Schnauzer's Weight

As your Schnauzer gets older, she will likely become less active. Like with humans, getting older and less active makes dogs more likely to put on weight.

HELPFUL TIP
Is My Dog Overweight?

Being overweight puts your pet at risk for a number of diseases and health complications. One way to determine if your dog is overweight is by using the body conditioning score for your dog's specific breed and comparing the visual appearance of your dog to the images provided. When in doubt, check with your vet for tips on maintaining a healthy body weight for your dog!

Obesity in Schnauzers can lead to a host of serious health problems, including pancreatitis, diabetes, joint issues, heart disease, back pain, and other issues. If your Schnauzer packs on some extra pounds, the key to getting those pounds off is the same as for humans: diet and exercise.

If your dog is not getting much exercise, start by taking her on short walks every day, possibly more than once a day.

You will also need to cut down on her food. If you've been giving her table scraps, stop. Switch to boiled, skinless white meat chicken in limited quantities as treats.

You should also look into a weight management food. As mentioned earlier in this chapter, a weight-management wet food may make your Schnauzer feel fuller because of the water content, which can help reduce her calorie intake more easily than just cutting down on food. You can also feed her twice a day rather than just once, so she feels like she's getting more food.

Finally, talk to your vet. In some cases, your vet may prescribe a special diet formula food until your Schnauzer takes off a few pounds.

Remember, with dogs, extra weight can lead to reduced quality and length of life. Find other ways to reward your pup beyond fattening treats and scraps, and you'll both be happier in the long run.

CHAPTER 15
Grooming your Schnauzer

"Their hair actually grows really long if not kept trimmed. The haircut really makes the dog. Miniature Schnauzers are often shaved when kept as pets, which typically creates a softer coat. For people who prefer the coarse coat that the breed calls for, a process called 'hand stripping' or 'rolling the coat' is used which keeps the dead hairs pulled out and allows for the new hair to grow in more easily."

KELLY ROBISON
Belle Vista Schnauzers

The Schnauzer Cut

Schnauzers should be groomed at least once every two months. Beyond just looking better, there are practical reasons why Schnauzers need haircuts. As the eyebrows grow out, they will start to cover your

*Photo Courtesy
of Ron Fazio*

Schnauzer's eyes, making it harder for her to see. She may have pieces of fur that mat together, which can pull on her skin and be uncomfortable. While this is a little gross, one of the biggest issues we've had when we've let our Schnauzer's hair get too long is that her feces will get caught in her fur—and that's no fun for either of us.

The traditional Schnauzer cut keeps your dog's fur on her body, head, and neck shorter, with more fur on the legs, rounded at the paws. The eyebrows and beards are kept longer. We go with an easier-to-maintain version that keeps her hair short all over, including her legs. While we still do the Schnauzer face (i.e., eyebrows and beard), we have them cut shorter. All of this is for practical reasons. We can go a little longer between cuts, the eyebrows don't get in her eyes as quickly, and Schnauzer beards get really messy, really fast.

While you can get clippers and try to do it yourself, I would really recommend finding a professional groomer. When choosing groomers, research their reputation, licenses, training, and so on. Also find out where they will house your dog during breaks. How many dogs do they work on at a time? I'd also talk to them about any treats they give. (I'll get into why more in the next chapter.) You may also be able to find a groomer that will come to your house. I have not tried that yet, but may soon.

Grooming takes a while because dogs need breaks between sessions. The fastest Puggles has ever had her hair done was two hours. It's not unusual for her to be gone four to six hours on grooming days.

Bathing and Brushing

Just like with everything else, it's best to start with brushing and bathing early on so your Schnauzer will get used to the process. (Doesn't mean she'll ever grow to like baths though!)

As I've mentioned, Schnauzers' beards get really dirty easily, especially if you're feeding her any kind of wet food or if she likes to dig in the yard. Schnauzers are prone to allergies and dry skin, so using the right shampoo is important. I would go with something that's gentle and hypoallergenic and made specifically for dogs. When giving a bath, you can do it indoors or outside, or some towns even have do-it-yourself dog-washing facilities. The biggest issue with doing it outside is the water temperature. Cold water is

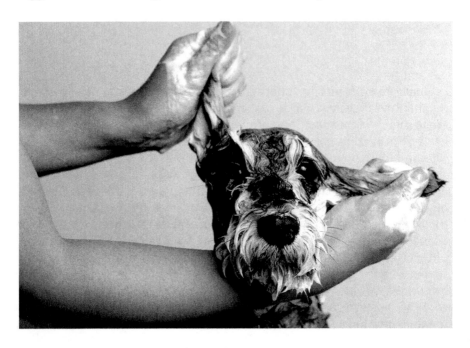

not so bad on a hot summer day, but can be problematic as it gets cooler. You'll need to have your supplies ready: dog shampoo, a comb or brush, something to use to pour the water on your dog (if you don't have a hose sprayer), and several towels.

I've always used the bathtub. You'll want the temperature to be pretty warm. At the animal shelter, they've taught us to make it hotter than I traditionally thought because a dog's body temperature is naturally warmer.

The first step is to get your dog thoroughly wet. If you don't have a hose sprayer in your tub, use a big cup and fill it with the running bathwater. You want to saturate your dog's fur.

Next, shampoo thoroughly, following the product's instructions. Be careful of sensitive areas, like the eyes. You can use a soft washcloth for cleaning her eyes and ears.

Photo Courtesy of Sunshine Herondale

Finally, rinse. Rinsing the body is not hard. Just use the sprayer or cup and dump clean water over your dog. The face, though, is a little trickier. I always save it for last, then cover Puggles' eyes and gently pour the water over her head. A washcloth can help as well. For her beard, I hold her muzzle, cover her nose, lift her face upward so that her nose is pointing toward the ceiling, then spray the water starting at the chin and down her neck.

When you finish rinsing, it's time to dry. I always empty the bathtub before I let Puggles out so I can start drying her while she's standing in the tub. When her fur is longer, it really retains water, so the drier I can get her before she steps out of the tub, the better. Once she's out of the tub, I grab more towels and dry her as much as I can before I let her run around the house. She is hyper when she finishes her bath! She runs and flops on everything—including furniture—to try to dry her fur some more. The good news is that at least she doesn't shed. I've had other breeds of dogs who left the tubs full of fur, then rubbed more fur on the furniture after their baths.

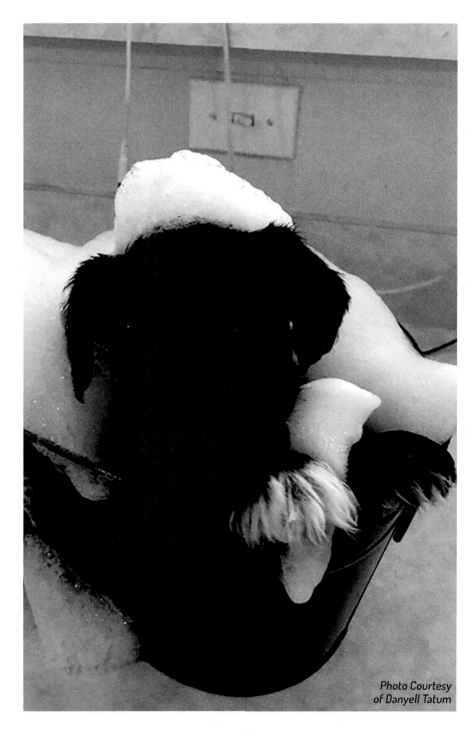

Photo Courtesy
of Danyell Tatum

Brushing your Schnauzer's fur at least once a week is also important to prevent matting. This removes the undercoat hair that has shed and helps keep it from getting caught in the topcoat and causing tangles as the hair gets longer. It can also help improve her circulation, and helps remove allergens that can bother her skin. Pat A. Hunt of Alpats Miniature Schnauzer adds, "If your Schnauzer is wearing a sweater in winter or a harness, that area will tangle and need to be brushed maybe daily."

For everyday grooming, you'll just need a bristle brush to remove dirt and allergens and help distribute the natural body oils throughout your Schnauzer's coat. A flea comb is good for not only detecting fleas but also breaking up matted hair and removing loose undercoat fur.

To brush, first find a comfortable spot where your Schnauzer can lie down. Speak gently to help calm her, then lay her on her side. Brush slowly and gently down one side, then roll her over to the other. If you come across matted fur, switch to the flea comb and gently try to work through it, being careful not to pull her skin. If it seems like too much, wait until a professional groomer can help.

Trimming Nails

Letting your Schnauzer's nails grow too long is not only painful, but it can actually cause serious issues. With time, long nails can lead to spine problems and weight issues as they will cause your dog to walk incorrectly and limit her movement.

If your dog's nails touch the ground, they are too long and need to be trimmed. The good news is when you take your dog for grooming, you can easily have her nails trimmed. If your Schnauzer goes on plenty of walks, that will help wear the nails down. Even so, nail grooming is key.

Here's how to trim your dog's nails:

- Gather the necessary supplies. You'll want to have dog clippers or scissors and a flashlight, plus styptic powder.

- Shine the flashlight on the nail. This makes it easier to see where the blood flow stops. (Darker nails are more difficult than white nails). You don't want to cut where the blood flows, which is called the quick. Cutting the quick is painful and can lead to infection.

- Carefully trim the nail. When trimming, always cut parallel to the bottom of the nail. You don't want to trim too high up, or you'll cause it to bleed.

- If you do cause the nail to bleed, press styptic powder or cornstarch on the nail to try to stop the bleeding. If the bleeding doesn't stop within about 30 minutes, call your vet.

Cleaning Ears and Eyes

FUN FACT
Standard Schnauzer

The wiry whiskers on the snout of the Standard Schnauzer may have had an important function in this breed's past; the whiskers would become matted together around the dog's face and acted as a barrier to protect against bites from the vermin that this breed was bred to hunt on farms in Germany.

Keeping your dog's eyes and ears cleaned is as important as keeping her bathed and groomed. Too much eye gunk can cause infection, as well as discomfort for your Schnauzer. Ears, too, can become infected if not cleaned regularly.

Your dog will naturally have some eye discharge that will collect primarily in the inside corner of her eyes. Getting that uncomfortable eye gunk out will help her feel better, protect against infections, and help prevent scratching her cornea. You can clean your dog's eyes by using a warm, wet washcloth or cotton ball, which will help soften the discharge. There are also eye washes designed especially for dogs. When wiping the eyes, make sure not to wipe across the eyeball itself, and be careful not to pull too hard.

Your Schnauzer's eyes should be bright and clear without discharge (except while sleeping). If her eyes appear red, swollen, or otherwise look different than normal, contact your veterinarian. Also watch out if your dog is pawing at her eyes or blinking more than normal.

You should also check your Schnauzer's ears weekly for odors or redness, which can mean there is an infection. At the shelter, we would sometimes get dogs with yeast infections in their ears. They had a distinctly sweet odor and would usually yelp if we touched them wrong. I even had a really sweet German Shepherd snap at me once (then I could tell he felt really bad about it afterward). If your dog ever yelps when you touch her ears, that may be an indicator that something is not right.

Finally, ear mites are common. They look like black dirt in your dog's ears and are really itchy. Contact your vet if you suspect mites.

To clean the ears, use a cotton ball dipped in mineral oil or a special ear cleaner for dogs. Gently wipe inside your dog's ears, but don't ever go deep into the ear canal. Also don't use things like alcohol or peroxide that may dry out the ears because that can cause problems.

Brushing Teeth

"Teeth should be professionally cleaned every 3 years as Schnauzers are prone to having tooth problems."

BARBARA DURRANCE
Show Stopper Schnauzers

Periodontal disease is extremely common in dogs over age three, which can be painful and compromise the integrity of their teeth. Allowing your dog to chew on things like bones, chew toys, and rawhides can help scrape excess plaque off her teeth, but it's still best to also brush your dog's teeth regularly. Ideally, you'll brush them every day, but doing it a minimum of three times a week is a reasonable goal. Again, it's best to start this right away when your dog is young. Here's how to get her used to teeth brushing:

- Start when your dog is calm.
- If your Schnauzer is small enough, hold her in your lap with her head facing away from you. You can also have your dog sit beside you.
- Use a soft cloth and wipe along her outer teeth, paying special attention to the gum line.
- After doing this a few separate times, your Schnauzer will be more used to you rubbing her teeth, which will make it easier to add toothpaste.
- Place a little dog toothpaste on your finger and let her taste it. DO NOT use human toothpaste as it is not safe for your dog to swallow. Also, do not use baking soda as it will upset the pH level in your dog's stomach.
- Next, add some of the toothpaste to your cloth and use the same process from before.
- Once your dog has done this a few times, you can use a toothbrush instead.

There are a variety of dog toothbrushes on the market, and you may want to try a few to find the one that works best for you. A lot of people prefer toothbrushes that slip over their fingers as opposed to those that resemble human toothbrushes.

Finally, you'll want to have your veterinarian check your Schnauzer's teeth annually. In some cases, you may need to have her teeth professionally cleaned for her protection and comfort.

CHAPTER 16
Basic Health Care

I n my experience volunteering at the animal shelter, too many people do not recognize the responsibility and expense that goes along with owning a dog. One of the most expensive and most important things that you must do for your Schnauzer is to protect her health. You are her family. Her guardian. And with that comes the need to take care of her physical needs.

Regular Vet Visits

When it comes to your Schnauzer, you really need to take her for an annual checkup, not just when she's feeling sick. Just like humans, dogs need wellness visits to help make sure there are no hidden health problems.

Photo Courtesy of Jeff Rangel

Routine visits, which usually happen at least once a year, let your vet see how your Schnauzer is growing and adapting as she ages. It can also help your vet identify problems early on, and early detection is key for more serious issues.

During your dog's checkup, the vet will typically look over your Schnauzer's skin, coat, mouth, paws, ears, eyes, belly, tail, etc. Your Schnauzer will also be tested for worms, including heartworms, from a stool sample and blood draw. Finally, if it's time, she'll need to get her vaccinations.

Protecting from Fleas and Ticks

With warmer weather comes two of the worst problems dogs regularly face: fleas and ticks. Both are parasites, and your Schnauzer needs to be protected against both.

Fleas

These tiny, wingless insects feed on the blood of animals, such as dogs and cats. Flea infestations are difficult because they can produce millions of offspring. If your dog tracks in fleas, it's not uncommon to find them jumping through your home's carpet and bedding. They're not picky. They will bite you too.

Fleas can sometimes be hard to spot on your dog. They prefer the abdomen, as well as the base of the tail and head. You may not see the fleas, but you may find their droppings, which look like patches of dirt or sand. Another obvious sign is if your dog is obsessively scratching. Without treatment, your dog may chew her fur off.

Itching is not the only problem that fleas can cause. Because they drink so much blood—15 times their own body weight—this can lead to anemia, especially in puppies. Furthermore, fleas can transmit worm eggs, which can cause additional health issues.

Ticks

These arachnids bury their heads under a dog's skin to feed. You can often tell if a tick has been there a while based on its size—the bigger it is, the more likely it's been feeding longer. While your dog may not feel a tick bite, ticks can carry a number of diseases, including Lyme Disease, and they need to be removed. Ticks can also be transferred from your dog to your family, so again, get rid of them when you see them.

When you remove a tick, you don't want to just pull it directly off your dog because its head will come off and stay embedded under your dog's skin. This can cause infection. Touching the tick's blood can also increase the risk of infection. It's best to wear rubber gloves for protection.

I've found it easiest to have another family member hold and pet Puggles when it's time to have a tick removed. When you remove the tick, do it carefully. Use tweezers by grasping the tick's body as closely as you can get to your dog's skin, then pull straight up, slowly and evenly. Make sure you remove the entire head to avoid chances of an infection. Drop the tick in alcohol to kill it afterward. You can also get tick-removal tools that are very inexpensive and work great. I find these easier to use.

Once the tick has been removed, keep an eye on your dog for any signs of a localized infection. Watch for symptoms like redness, inflammation, or scratching. If you notice symptoms, call your vet.

Photo Courtesy
of Robin Boersner

If your dog has fleas or ticks, there are a few important things you need to do. First, you'll want to wash your dog using a flea and tick shampoo. Follow the instructions carefully, which typically include leaving the shampoo on for at least a minimum amount of time necessary to help kill the parasites. Afterward, use a brush to help remove any dead fleas and ticks stuck on your dog's fur.

There are a number of over-the-counter flea and tick preventatives, but I suggest talking to your vet as some OTC treatments can be toxic to cats and humans. Veterinary treatments are more expensive, but they are also safer and more effective than what you'll find at the pet store.

Because fleas and ticks are brought in from outdoors, you'll want to treat your yard for these parasites as well, whether it's on your own or through a professional pest control company. The same holds true for inside your home if you've had an infestation. If you do it yourself, make sure to follow the instructions, cover food and other items, and protect your pets.

> ## HELPFUL TIP
> ### Ticks and Lyme Disease
>
>
>
> April is National Prevent Lyme Disease in Dogs month, which is fitting because, in many parts of the United States, ticks begin to be active in early spring. In some parts of the US, however, ticks are active all year round. Prevention is the easiest way to keep your dog healthy and free from Lyme disease. Talk to your vet about flea and tick control options and treatments.

Worms

Dogs typically get worms by ingesting them or from fleas. While the idea of worms is gross, it's certainly not uncommon. But it needs to be treated.

If your Schnauzer has gastrointestinal issues like diarrhea, vomiting, unexplained weight loss, a distended belly, or belly tenderness, it could be from worms. Other signs include poor coat appearance, dehydration, lethargy, and bloody stools. You'll need to get your dog checked out by your vet.

Let's look at the different kinds of worms:

1. **Roundworms** – There are two different types of roundworms, *Toxocara canis (T. canis) and Toxascaris leonina*. The first kind, T. canis, can be transmitted to unborn puppies through their mother, and can be passed on to humans as well. That's one key reason newborn puppies need proper veterinary care. Left untreated, roundworms can hinder growth and even lead to death in severe cases. Roundworms are detected through a stool sample.

2. Hookworms – These intestinal parasites can cause anemia or worse, especially in puppies, if not properly treated. They are tiny worms—about one-eighth of an inch long—that attach to a dog's intestinal wall and ingest a lot of blood. Puppies can become infected through their mother's milk if she has hookworms. Dogs can also get worms from ingesting dirt or from sniffing dog feces that have been infected.

3. Tapeworms – These are another type of intestinal parasite that can be ingested primarily by eating fleas. Once the tapeworm egg hatches inside the dog's body, the worm attaches to the intestinal lining. You can sometimes see tapeworms in stool, or if your dog is scooting on her butt, it may indicate tapeworms, and you should visit your vet for treatment.

4. Whipworms – Dogs get whipworms by ingesting contaminated soil. These worms live in the large intestine and colon, where they can survive up to five years. In mild cases, they don't always lead to symptoms, but more severe cases can cause diarrhea, anemia, weight loss, and inflammation. Because they are such a hardy type of parasite, treatment typically lasts for three months. Be aware that false negatives are not uncommon when checking for whipworms, so you may need to have your Schnauzer tested more than once if she continues to have symptoms.

5. Heartworms – This is the most serious form of worm problems, but it is also the most preventable. Heartworms are transmitted through mosquitoes, then they grow and multiply through the heart. Heartworm

Photo Courtesy
of Anttu Suhonen

preventatives are essential. They may seem expensive, but they are nowhere near as expensive as treatment, and treatment also requires keeping your dog confined to a small space to limit her activity while the heartworms die and are removed from the body. Left untreated, heartworms can clog a dog's circulatory system and eventually lead to heart damage and death.

Vaccinations

Keeping your dog vaccinated is one of the most important things that you can do for her in that it can protect her from dangerous, sometimes deadly diseases. There are some vaccinations that are necessary for every dog, and others that are optional. Let's start with the necessary vaccines. The first four are usually given together. Distemper and parvo vaccines can be started on puppies as young as six weeks, but the other two should not start until around 10 to 12 weeks old. Then boosters can be given every two to four weeks up until 16 to 20 weeks, depending on what your vet recommends.

- **Distemper** – Distemper is a highly contagious virus that's similar to the measles virus. It's a widespread infection that attacks throughout the body, making it difficult to treat and fight, and is often lethal. I had to have a puppy put down for distemper when I was a child.

- **Parvovirus** – Parvo is a highly infectious gastrointestinal condition that mostly occurs in puppies before they are vaccinated. We've had a few parvo outbreaks at the shelter. It's a nasty disease that spreads very quickly. Multiple puppies have had to be put down at the shelter because of parvo, and when it hits, we've had to limit guests being able to interact with the other dogs for fear of transferring the disease to dogs that had not yet been fully vaccinated. It causes an infectious gastrointestinal illness in puppies and young dogs, and without treatment, it is potentially deadly.

The good news is that if caught early enough, it may be treatable. In fact, we fostered a puppy that was brought into the shelter right after they had a parvo outbreak. We took him home to foster, hoping to keep him safe. But that night, he started throwing up multiple times. We took him to the vet first thing the next morning, and he tested positive for parvo. However, after putting him on fluids and antidiarrheal medicine, the puppy was ready to come back to our house 48 hours later, good as new. Thank goodness Puggles was up-to-date on her vaccines! (We couldn't have fostered if she wasn't.) After that experience, we were not allowed to foster another puppy for two years due to the potential risk of Parvo.

- **Adenovirus** – Also known as canine hepatitis, this virus is found in both feces and saliva and causes vomiting, diarrhea, and fever. It can be fatal, but it is preventable through vaccination.
- **Rabies** – If you've seen the classic movie Old Yeller, then you know you don't want your dog to get rabies! Rabies is a lethal but preventable disease that affects the nervous system. If a rabid animal bites someone or another animal, rabies can be passed on. Most states require rabies vaccinations by law.

This next part is kind of graphic, but I'm going to share anyway. In addition to being required by law, know that if your dog bites someone, has to be put down, and has not been vaccinated against rabies, veterinarians or shelters are required by law to cut off the deceased dog's head and test her brain. They've had to do it at the animal shelter, and it's awful. You don't want that to happen to your dog!

In most cases, puppies get their initial rabies shot around 16 weeks of age. They should not get it before 12 weeks. Then a booster will be needed in a year. There are annual or three-year shot options available.

There are also other shots that are considered optional. These include the following:

- **Bordetella bronchiseptica and canine parainfluenza virus** – This is for kennel cough, and is typically required before boarding your dog.
- **Leptospira** – This is for a type of bacteria often found in mud and standing water. The bacteria can cause liver and kidney damage. This shot is primarily for dogs that will be used for hunting.
- **Borrelia burgdorferi (Lyme Disease)** – This shot helps protect against tick-transmitted Lyme Disease.
- **Canine Influenza Virus-H3N8** – Yes, this is to protect your dog from the flu. If you or your dog are around other dogs a lot, such as at a dog park or doggy daycare, you may want to consider getting this vaccine. Because we volunteered at the animal shelter (pre-COVID-19), we got the vaccine for Puggles last winter.
- **Allergy Shots** – Schnauzers are prone to allergies, which can cause a lot of itching. We have gotten Puggles an allergy shot most years. However, this is a steroid shot, and it had some adverse effects this past year, probably because she is now over 11 years old. The reaction can imitate pancreatitis, and her symptoms started a week after her shot, so we really aren't sure if it's the shot or pancreatitis that's been causing recent gastrointestinal issues for her.

Spaying and Neutering

As a volunteer at our local animal shelter, I've seen hundreds of stray dogs that were found or relinquished, never to be reunited with their owners. I've also seen puppies adopted out, then brought back a few months later because owners did not realize the work involved in raising a puppy. As such, I cannot in good conscience write this book without stressing that unless you plan to breed your Schnauzer, you should please have your dog spayed or neutered.

Beyond the problem of full shelters, spaying and neutering is actually better for your dog. Just like with humans, when female dogs go into heat, it's messy. Having your female dog's ovaries removed gets rid of those heat cycles and can protect her from some serious health problems like breast cancer and uterine infections.

For males, getting your dog neutered helps get rid of some behavior problems. Most of the dogs that are brought to the shelter are males that are unneutered, which makes sense because they are more likely to get out because they have the urge to mate. (The females who are picked up are often in heat.) Unneutered males are also more aggressive.

Like with females, having your male dog neutered will also protect against potential health issues. These include having an enlarged prostate gland and testicular cancer.

Spaying and neutering are simple processes with little risk. It's a simple surgery. Some animal shelters have programs to help cover the cost. For example, our local animal shelter worked with certain vets who would spay or neuter for just $25. In fact, that's how we ended up finding our awesome vet that we've now used for over a decade.

Natural Supplements for Dogs

Like with humans, natural supplements are growing in popularity. While they may be good for your dogs, you should know that unlike medication, natural supplements are not regulated by a governing body, which means you should use caution when choosing which ones to give your Schnauzer. Like with anything, it's best to talk to your vet first and then to buy from a reputable brand.

Here are some supplements that may be helpful for your Schnauzer:

- **Glucosamine** – This amino sugar is naturally found in the fluid surrounding the joints. For supplements, glucosamine either is removed

*Photo Courtesy
of Ann Schuh*

from shells in shellfish or made in a lab. In older dogs, glucosamine may help with arthritis or other joint pain. Glucosamine supplements usually also contain chondroitin sulfate, which is naturally found in the connective tissue of cartilage and bones.

- **Antioxidants** – In dogs, antioxidant supplements are believed to help with certain aspects of aging, particularly with cognitive function. Antioxidants also can help reduce inflammation and other aging problems.

- **Fish Oil** – These supplements contain omega-3 fatty acids, which may help with skin allergies, as well as improving coat quality. Fish oil may also reduce inflammation.

- **Probiotics** – These microscopic bacteria help with digestion, as well as fight yeast.

How Does Pet Insurance Work?

Vet bills can be expensive. Emergency vet bills can be outrageous.

A couple of years ago, Puggles went outside around 10 p.m. and shortly after, I heard her yelping like I've never heard before. She was bitten by a copperhead. We had to take her to the emergency vet, where we were given two options: Benadryl and a steroid shot for $400 or an overnight stay and antivenom for over $2,000. We did the Benadryl. (She was fine once the pain finally subsided.)

While at the emergency vet, I overheard them talking to someone whose dog was going into surgery. The family was asked if they wanted the doctors to try to revive the dog if things went south. It would cost an extra $1,000 to perform CPR. Ugh. Can you imagine having to make that decision?

That's why pet insurance may be a smart option.

A number of companies offer pet insurance these days, and like health insurance, there are different plan options. You pay a monthly fee that's determined based on the age, type, and health of your Schnauzer. Some plans have a deductible that you must meet. Others will only pay a certain percentage of bills.

In most situations, your vet will not bill the insurance. You have to pay the bill, then submit it to the insurance for reimbursement. When you are looking at plans, look to see what is covered and what is not. Some insurance companies will reject claims if you are not up-to-date on vaccinations, etc. The good news is some plans cover wellness visits. Finally, some plans have a maximum amount they will cover per year.

Photo Courtesy
of Dagne Sereičikiene

CHAPTER 17
Advanced Schnauzer Health and Aging Dog Care

A few weeks ago, I took Puggles to the groomer. When I picked her up, I remember thinking, "Wow, she looks like she's put on some weight!" When she came home, she lay quietly by the door, acting like she was upset with me. But in the years we've had her, she's never been upset with me, even for a moment.

That evening, she couldn't get comfortable on our bed. I could hear her stomach gurgling as she struggled to find the right position. She also passed gas, which she doesn't do very often. Then after about an hour, she started vomiting—a lot. Eventually she settled in and fell asleep. But when I went downstairs, I realized she had come down in the middle of the night and had gone diarrhea all over the living room rug. That never happens! She usually wakes me up if she needs to go potty.

I took her to the vet the next day, where bloodwork confirmed my fear. Pancreatitis.

Photo Courtesy of Sabrina Roybal

What is Pancreatitis?

Putting it in basic terms, pancreatitis is an inflammation of the pancreas, the organ that releases enzymes during digestion. In a normal working pancreas, the enzymes do not become active until they reach the small intestine. With pancreatitis, the enzymes start working the moment they are released, which causes inflammation and potential damage to the pancreas and other organs and tissues.

Unfortunately, Schnauzers are highly prone to pancreatitis, especially as they get older.

HELPFUL TIP
Signs of Hearing Loss

Hearing loss may be a health issue that your dog deals with as he ages. One sign of hearing loss is a lack of responsiveness to his name, loud noises, or squeaky toys. Hearing loss can be caused by a variety of things, including but not limited to your dog's age. It's important to talk to your vet if you notice hearing loss in your dog to rule out any other underlying conditions.

That's why I've stressed throughout this book the importance of watching your dog's fat intake. The top reason for pancreatitis is too much fatty food.

Pancreatitis symptoms vary, and it's important to recognize your Schnauzer's upset tummy may be something more serious. Watch for signs such as:

- Diarrhea
- Repeated vomiting
- Swollen/bloated abdomen
- Hunched back
- Problems getting comfortable
- Loss of appetite
- Dehydration
- Fever.

To determine whether your dog has pancreatitis, the vet will check for a fever and do a physical examination, checking her stomach, heart, and gums. The vet will also want to take a blood test to check for pancreatic enzymes. Your dog's history will also come into play.

Pancreatitis can be acute or chronic. Acute pancreatitis comes on seemingly out of nowhere, like with Puggles. Chronic pancreatitis develops over time, often without symptoms. Both acute and chronic are painful and can be mild or severe, which can be potentially life-threatening.

While there's no cure for pancreatitis, you may be able to manage it. Early intervention is important to prevent complications. Generally, treatment may consist of pain and/or nausea meds, intravenous fluids, and changing your Schnauzer's diet.

In our case, Puggles was given fluids under the skin and a prescription low fat food to eat for the next several days. Since that time, we have eliminated table scraps, treats, and bones, and switched her to a lower fat dog food. She has occasionally gotten hold of cat food (I caught her on top of our table eating it!) and some other food she dug out of the trash, and while she's not had as severe an episode again, she has had bouts of diarrhea each time.

If your Schnauzer has pancreatitis, talk to your vet about supplements that might be beneficial. Some recommend digestive enzymes that have pancreatin to help reduce pancreatic secretion. Despite its high fat content, fish oil may actually be beneficial in that it can help lower blood lipid levels. In some human studies, probiotics were found to make pancreatitis worse, so be cautious with those.

The bad news is that pancreatitis doesn't go away. Once it hits, there's a high chance it will happen again. That's why switching your Schnauzer's diet, providing smaller meals more than once a day, watching her weight, and being aware of warning signs is important.

Mild cases, such as what Puggles had, typically have a good prognosis, but more severe cases can lead to complications.

Other Genetic Traits Found in Schnauzers

"The most common genetic problem in the breed is a strong tendency to form different types of bladder stones, usually struvite or calcium oxalate stones. Using the correct food can make a big difference."

RHONDA SMITH
Heavenly Miniature Schnauzer

While pancreatitis is the most common concern for Schnauzers, there are other conditions that these dogs are predisposed to having:

1. **Skin allergies** – Also referred to as "atopy," this condition primarily affects the feet, tummy, ears, and back toward the tail. When Puggles gets especially itchy, we get her an allergy shot, which is a steroid shot that lasts a couple of months each time. Talk to your vet about options.

2. **Diabetes** – While any dog breed can become diabetic, it's a bigger concern for Schnauzers. Symptoms include increased drinking, eating, urinating, and possible weight loss. Treatment requires dedication, as diabetic Schnauzers typically require daily insulin injections and special diets. The good news is that with proper treatment, diabetic Schnauzers can still have long, happy lives.

3. **Cushing's Disease (hyperadrenocorticism)** – This is caused when the adrenal glands malfunction, and they produce too much steroid hormones. The test for Cushing's is quite expensive, and so is the treatment. Unlike pancreatitis, which can come out of nowhere, Cushing's develops slowly. Early signs include increased appetite and thirst, urinating more frequently, developing a potbelly, hair loss, and thin skin.

4. **Portosystemic Shunt (PSS)** – This is a liver disorder that Schnauzers are more likely to have than most breeds, where some of the blood supply that should reach the liver is diverted. With PSS, dogs can't remove toxins from their blood as needed. Some cases can be fixed with diet and medication, while others require surgery.

5. **Heart disease** – Schnauzers are prone to a variety of types of heart disease, especially as they get older. Heart failure is the number one cause of death for older Schnauzers. Early detection, along with proper medication, can often extend your Schnauzer's life significantly. Keeping your dog's teeth cleaned and ensuring she maintains a healthy weight also plays a big role in preventing heart disease.

Photo Courtesy of Shaunda Mckillip

6. **Bleeding disorders** – Schnauzers are prone to some fairly rare blood diseases. Hemolytic anemia and thrombocytopenia are when the immune system starts attacking the dog's red blood cells, causing her to become weak, lethargic, and anemic. Another blood condition, Von Willebrand's Disease, is a blood-clotting disorder that's fairly common in Schnauzers.

7. **Kidney disease** – Glomerulonephropathy is an inherited form of kidney disease that can eventually lead a dog's kidneys to fail, even at a young age. Schnauzers are more prone to developing kidney disorders and bladder stones than many other breeds.

8. **Schnauzer Comedo Syndrome** – This skin disorder is only found in Schnauzers and produces skin lesions on their back. It's caused by an inherited defect in the hair follicles. Unless they become infected, these lesions are not painful and do not need to be biopsied. Puggles gets them from time to time. If they do become infected, your Schnauzer may need to have the lesions cleaned with special shampoos, astringents, and may require antibiotics.

Preventing Illness and Injury in Your Senior Schnauzer

Puggles is now 11.5 years old. It wasn't until about six months ago that her age began to start showing, which is about right. Small dogs, like Miniature Schnauzers, often aren't really considered seniors until they turn around 10 or 11. Standard Schnauzers are considered seniors around age eight, and Giant Schnauzers are considered seniors around the age of six.

As dogs get older, they get slower and are more prone to weight gain and joint pain—a lot like humans. As your Schnauzer gets older, you'll need to really watch her weight. Again, fatty foods are always bad for Schnauzers, but especially as they get older. Senior dog foods are designed to be lower in fat and have fewer calories.

While exercise is always important for your Schnauzer, she'll probably need to go for shorter, slower walks than when she was younger. Her energy level is going to be less than when she was younger, and her joints will ache more.

As your dog gets older, her immune system will also weaken. She may lose hearing (Puggles' hearing has greatly diminished recently) and develop cataracts.

For all these reasons and more, it's especially important to keep up with your vet visits, possibly once every six months instead of just once a year. This will help your vet catch any illnesses early and potentially prolong and improve your Schnauzer's quality of life.

Grooming Your Senior

As we already covered earlier in this book, Schnauzers require regular grooming. This is not just haircuts, but also caring for teeth, nails, and skin. Because they are less active, senior Schnauzers need their nails trimmed more often to prevent discomfort and problems walking.

Older dogs get cold and hot easier, so it's especially important to take care of your Schnauzer's coat. Keeping her fur tangle-free by regularly brushing will allow her coat to insulate better than when she has matted hair. When brushing your senior, use a softer brush. Your Schnauzer may develop some tender bumps as she ages, and you'll want to be gentle so as not to hurt her.

When bathing your dog at home, use a nonslip mat in the tub to prevent injuries. Older skin is drier and flakier, so use a dog shampoo that is designed for skin conditions, then make sure you rinse thoroughly. To keep your Schnauzer from getting cold, use towels to absorb as much water as possible from her fur. You can then use a hair dryer on warm (not hot) to dry her thoroughly.

Nutrition for Seniors

As your dog gets older, she will lose muscle mass, which can weaken her system, making it harder to recover from illness and injury. That's why increasing your Schnauzer's protein intake is important, and a minimum of 25 percent of all calories should come from protein in senior dogs.

Senior dogs can be more prone to constipation, and fiber may help regulate glucose. Increase fiber in your dog's diet, too, but use caution. Too much fiber can lead to diarrhea, bloating, and other gastrointestinal issues.

Senior Schnauzers may need a low-sodium diet to protect against heart or kidney problems and hypertension.

Finally, older dogs often have rotting or missing teeth, which makes eating more difficult. Switching to wet food is often a good choice for older dogs. It also helps provide more fluids. Your best bet is to switch to a senior dog food. Ask your vet for recommendations.

Older dogs get dehydrated faster, especially if they have kidney disease or other problems like pancreatitis that make them urinate more frequently. Make sure you provide cool, fresh, clean water at all times.

Providing Special Accommodations

Senior dogs often have joint issues and/or develop arthritis that make mobility more difficult. As your Schnauzer ages, she may have a harder time getting on furniture (if allowed), climbing stairs, and even maneuvering hardwood floors.

At a fundraiser for the shelter where I volunteer, I bought Puggles a small set of doggy stairs to help her get on the bed. That was possibly the best $25 I've ever spent. (Note: they usually run closer to $50, but that would have been well worth it as well.) I highly recommend getting some doggy stairs if you have a Miniature Schnauzer.

If your dog has trouble going up and down your stairs as she gets older, you may want to purchase or build a doggy ramp. If you have hardwood floors, consider adding some rugs to help keep your senior Schnauzer from sliding. Her arthritis will thank you.

Make sure your dog has a comfortable dog bed. Because she will get colder easier than when she was younger, provide some extra blankets.

Finally, if your Schnauzer loses her eyesight, she will have a harder time maneuvering around your house. Make sure not to leave things out that can get in her way, and don't rearrange the furniture.

Saying Goodbye

I've always said that Puggles will live forever, and as much as I want to believe that, I'm starting to realize that it's not true. I've had nine dogs in my life, and they've all been special in their own way, but none has been as special as Puggles. It's going to hurt terribly when she is gone.

Volunteering at the shelter has helped me learn to let go, mostly as dogs I love are adopted, and I know I won't see them again. The shelter where I volunteer is not a no-kill shelter, but they've not had to put a dog down to overcrowding in over a decade. They have, however, had to put a few down due to health issues.

One especially sweet incident involved Roger, a senior pit bull who was at the shelter for about four months. At first, he scared me because he would bark when I got near his cage, but I soon figured out he just wanted attention. Then I realized he was just a sweet, gentle old man who loved belly rubs and giving kisses.

Roger developed a tumor on his belly while at the shelter. We had it biopsied, and it was cancer. They continued to let him live at the shelter until it became obvious he wasn't feeling good, and it was time to put him out of his pain.

The shelter called to let me and my daughter know. They moved him to the back room where it was quiet, and we made him a special cage filled with pillows and blankets. The staff bought him a Sam's rotisserie chicken as a special treat, although he didn't feel like eating much of it. We petted him, sang songs, and loved him for a few hours. Then at the end of the day, we said goodbye, and the staff gently, lovingly put him to sleep. He died knowing that despite being a stray, he was loved.

That's how I would encourage you to let go when it's time—by spending quality time with your Schnauzer, then letting her gently fall asleep, knowing she was loved.

Sadly, pet owners often have to face a heart-wrenching decision: do you prolong your dog's life when she's hurting or do you let her go? Your vet may guide you in the decision, but the choice is ultimately up to you. Veterinarians can provide you with your dog's prognosis and give an idea of how long she could live and how her quality of life may be.

When making the gut-wrenching decision, here are some things to think about, looking at long-term, not just temporary symptoms:

- How much is your dog hurting? Is she showing signs of pain such as panting, whining, decreased appetite, reluctance to move, or the inability to get comfortable?
- Is she drinking like she should? Whether she's drinking too little or much more than normal can be telling of an underlying condition.

- Is she able to eat, or is she refusing food?
- Is she struggling with urinary or fecal incontinence, and if so, is she able to move out of the mess?
- Does she seem happy? Is she still able to perform her favorite activities? Is she acting depressed, such as isolating herself from her family?
- Can she still move comfortably? Is she struggling with severe arthritis or other mobility issues that cannot be treated with medicine? Can she walk without help?
- Does she have more good days or bad days? If the answer is bad, then it may be time to let your dog go peacefully, rather than force her to wait until her body gives out on its own.

Photo Courtesy of Kay Jones

What to Expect

If you're able, I highly recommend being there with your dog when she's put down. This will help comfort her and will provide you with closure and the time to say goodbye.

Your vet will walk you through the process so that you know what is happening. He may give your Schnauzer a sedative to help her relax before giving the euthanasia medication. Most vets use pentobarbital, which is a seizure medication that quickly shuts down the heart and brain within a couple of minutes. The medication is typically given through an IV in a dog's leg.

Be prepared. Your Schnauzer may not fully close her eyes, especially if a sedative isn't given first. She may urinate or defecate, and you may even see her twitch as she takes her final breath. This can be upsetting, but know that it's normal and she doesn't feel any pain. She will be at peace, and her last memory will be of her loving family surrounding her.

Once she is gone, your vet can handle the body; you can have her cremated; you can bury her at home, or there may be a pet cemetery in your area.

Allow yourself time to grieve. Your Schnauzer is a member of your family, and losing her is going to hurt. It takes time to recover.

You may want to find a way to memorialize her, like holding a small memorial service or planting a tree in her favorite spot. If you have children, this can help them find closure. There are a variety of pet memorial ideas and suppliers online as well.

Finally, remember that pets are an important part of life. Give yourself time to grieve before you get another pet. While you may be tempted to never get another dog, I hope you will do so eventually. You aren't replacing your lost Schnauzer. You're adding a new family member with a unique personality. And you're giving another dog a loving home.

A Final Word

I have had nine dogs over the course of my 50 years on Earth, each one unique and special. But I can honestly say I've never had a dog that has touched my heart or loved me as much as my Miniature Schnauzer, Puggles.

I had no idea that day I brought her home as a stray how she would impact my life. I tell her every day that she is my best friend, and I mean it.

Schnauzers love their families like no dog I've seen before, and Puggles has become an incredibly important member of ours. Take the information in this book to heart, apply it to your daily life, and I can assure you your journey with your Schnauzer will be life changing.

Printed in Great Britain
by Amazon

20518563R00093